WORKING SPACE

Entrance to Milwaukee Center, showing lobby (above in archway) and Powerhouse Theater to the left.

WORKING SPACE

The Milwaukee Repertory Theater

Builds a Home

SARA O'CONNOR AND SHERRILL MYERS

Afterword by John Dillon

THEATRE COMMUNICATIONS GROUP

Copyright © 1992 by Sara O'Connor and Sherrill Myers
Afterword copyright © 1992 by John Dillon

Working Space is published by Theatre Communications Group, Inc.,
355 Lexington Ave., New York, NY 10017.

Working Space is supported in part by a grant from the Design Arts Program of the National Endowment for the Arts.

The photographs on pages ii, 90, 95, 99–108 are copyright © 1992 by John Nienhuis. All other photographs and illustrations are courtesy of the Milwaukee Repertory Theater and Beckley/Myers Architects.

O'Connor, Sara.
Working Space : the Milwaukee Repertory Theater builds a home /
Sara O'Connor and Sherrill Myers ; afterword by John Dillon.—1st ed.
ISBN 1-55936-033-X
1. Milwaukee Repertory Theater.   2. Theater architecture—Wisconsin—
Milwaukee.   3. Milwaukee (Wis.)—Buildings, structures, etc.   I. Myers, Sherrill.
II. Title.
NA6835.M55M556   1992
725′.822′0977595—dc20   91-20250
                                                        CIP

Design and composition by The Sarabande Press

First Edition, September 1992

Contents

THE BUILDING OF A THEATER:
"Take Fifteen Years and Call Me in the Morning"
Sara O'Connor

1

PHILOSOPHY:
On Architecture
Sherrill Myers

65

AFTERWORD
John Dillon

91

THE SPACE IN USE:
Comments From the Company

99

Original East Wells Street power plant.

THE BUILDING OF
A THEATER:

"Take Fifteen Years
and Call Me in the Morning"

SARA O'CONNOR

First Questions and Process

It all began innocently enough in 1978. I was invited to join a group of managers from other established theater companies at a session being held at the Guthrie Theater, where they would explain their long-range plan and urge a similar process upon us.

It was clear that this long-range planning, becoming so fashionable, was a good idea. However, I approached it somewhat warily, as the only "planning session" I had attended up to that time had been one instigated by the board of the Cincinnati Playhouse in the Park in 1971, and the major fallout from that meeting had been to let the artistic director go.

Determined to approach the process in a more thorough and positive manner here at the Milwaukee Repertory Theater, in 1979 we put together a long-range planning committee well balanced between board, company members and friends of the theater from the community.

One of the areas of concern which emerged from our discussion was that of facilities. There was strong feeling that our home in the Performing Arts Center (PAC) was inadequate on many fronts: lack of working space, poor light, overcrowding, separation of work areas which made communication difficult, inadequate backstage area, inadequate lobby space and public restroom facilities. In addition, the Milwaukee Rep had operated since 1974 a 99-seat second stage, the Court Street Theater, in a warehouse space about half a mile from the Rep's major home. An annual revival of *A Christmas Carol* at the 1376-seat Pabst Theater had begun in 1976.

Touring productions were going out to the Upper Midwest. Eleven productions a year were being rehearsed in a single windowless rehearsal hall in the basement of the PAC, plus borrowed floors of as-yet-unrented space in a new office tower three blocks away. There was no paint shop, so the Court Street Theater was used, and an annual search was mounted for temporary paint space when we needed to use the Court Street Theater as a theater.

The most urgent problem was adequate production space, and a temporary solution was found by renting space for the scene and paint shops in a new industrial building on the south side of the city. This allowed us to move the prop shop from its tiny quarters to the old PAC scene shop. Of course, all this also meant a great deal of trucking, and isolated the scene and paint shops from the rest of the theater.

With this temporary Band-Aid placed over one problem, we were able to turn to the big picture. Could we sufficiently alter and improve the situation we were in, or must we build a new theater?

At this point, fortune smiled upon the Milwaukee Repertory Theater, in the form of Beckley/Myers Architects. I had had some contact with Sherrill Myers and Bob Beckley a year or two previously, at a time when I was serving on the board of Theatre X, Milwaukee's premier experimental theater company. Bob and Sherrill had helped Theatre X prepare an application to the Design Arts program of the National Endowment for the Arts for assistance in planning renovation for a building. That application was not funded, but Sherrill, Bob and I got to know one another in the process.

They now offered to be of assistance to the Rep in whatever way they could. This generous offer opened the way for us to make a thorough examination of the process upon which we might be embarking. On the national scene, there were a number of questions to be considered:

1. What choices had been available to other theaters who had recently completed construction? Renovation of existing theatrical structures, conversion of older buildings originally used for other than theatrical purposes, the construction of new buildings from scratch?
2. What sort of planning and design process had they followed?
3. How had they financed the project?
4. How well did the completed building meet their needs?

Back at home, we needed to take a sharply considered look at the level of our own need to move. Was it genuinely compelling or simply a seductive vision of grander quarters? If we moved, what structures in the downtown area would lend themselves to a successful conversion?

I had another troubling question into which I hoped our research would provide some insight. Would the current and ongoing artistic aspirations of the company have to take a back seat for a number of years to the immense pressures generated by the construction and funding of a new home? I was fresh from the daunting and saddening experience of flying to Indianapolis to serve as an emergency consultant to the Indiana Repertory Theatre, where the artistic director had been fired by the executive committee as a result of stress and staff conflict directly attributable to the pressures of constructing their new theater. I didn't want that to happen to us. A new building would be useless if it destroyed the company's artistic integrity.

Together, Sherrill, Bob and I designed a project to give us at least some answers to our most pressing concerns, and an NEA Design Arts research grant sent Bob and Sherrill on visits to nine theater companies nationwide, in various stages of completion of, or preparation for, new facilities. Some fifty other theaters responded to questionnaires about needs.

The Beckley/Myers report, known as the *Theater Facilities Impact Study*, took nearly two years to complete and had two volumes:

Volume I: Theater Facilities: Guidelines and Strategies
This document contained the results of their nationwide search and covered both architectural design conclusions and some shrewd observations concerning the manner in which projects had been generated, carried out and funded.

Volume II: MRT Facilities: Analysis and Recommendations
This volume took on a thorough, detailed analysis of the MRT, its rhythm of production, its schedule, its channels of communication, its programmatic goals, its artistic philosophy and its organizational personality. In addition, Beckley/Myers carried out a detailed analysis of some half-dozen structures in the downtown area and assessed their suitability as a new home for the MRT.

Accepted by the MRT board in 1982, the Beckley/Myers' study soon received two richly deserved awards, one for research excellence from the National Endowment for the Arts, and a citation under the annual awards program of *Progressive Architecture* magazine.

The *Theater Facilities Impact Study* was useful to us in a number of ways, but at this point I would like to turn to a description of the process through which we arrived at the analysis and recommendations in *Volume II*. An understanding of that process is critical to an understanding of the philosophy which informed the project from beginning to end.

Theater is commonly referred to as a collaborative process, and we who work in it are sometimes heard to lay claim for it as an amalgam of all that's most exciting in the other, more singular, artforms. The strengths of a good creative collaboration are readily apparent in the best theatrical presentations.

As a managing director who came to the theater through the creative end, as actor and director, I tend to view the whole theater company as a collaborative process aimed at producing seasons of artistic work. Such process does not necessarily mean collective decision-making, and ultimately in a theater like ours the course is set by the artistic and managing directors; but collaboration brings great strengths to the setting and accomplishing of goals.

It was MRT's long-standing tendency to involve as many people as possible in order to get the most complete picture which meshed so well with Beckley/Myers' philosophy of creating facilities by allowing the users to become involved in the design process. This commitment on their part gave them the patience to engage in the long, exceedingly time-consuming process which resulted in a serious under-standing of how a theater company like ours *really* operates. One of the more humorous, but totally accurate, realizations was the "ball-of-twine" theory of organi-zation, which describes a theater company not as a pyramidal structure, but as an intricately interrelated organism in which each segment relates in a multiple fashion to many other segments.

We have since developed a computer model for our organizational structure which shows the relationships without the perception of tangle created by the twine theory, yet the ball of twine remains the most accurate depiction.

To use every piece of string making up our ball, we set up a series of voluntary discussion groups; anyone in the organization could participate and bring his or her creativity to bear on every question about the functional needs of a theater company. For nearly a year, a board in the green room in the basement of the Performing Arts Center displayed a rough outline of a building created by different-colored pieces of construction paper representing various spaces necessary to the smooth functioning of a theater. They were moved around, rearranged, reshaped, grew larger or smaller at every meeting as we struggled to create the right set of relationships for a successful working environment.

As we progressed, skillfully guided by the architects, who kept notes, raised

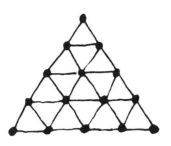

apparent organizational structure   *real organizational structure*

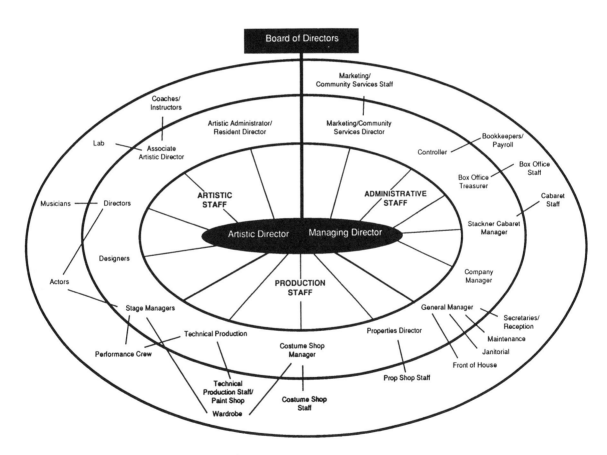

Computer model of organizational structure.

Colored paper cutouts diagramming potential spatial relationships.

issues, forced the facing of questions and sorted through all our wide-ranging ideas, several general principles assumed importance. They were:

1. The actual spaces should be as well-lighted, well-equipped and efficient as possible.
2. The location of each space in relation to other areas was of fundamental importance. The traffic pattern created by our working and information-sharing needs was becoming paramount.
3. The spaces should be human-sized and made for people to inhabit. The building was to be beautiful, but it was to make people comfortable, rather than overwhelm them with its grandeur.

The architects used questionnaires and kept cards and notes. But it cannot be overemphasized that their knowledge was primarily gained through direct discussions with company members and direct observation of work as it occurred in *all* areas of the theater.

This process not only gave Beckley/Myers a wealth of knowledge in the workings of a permanent theater company shared by few other architects, but it also—and this was my fervent hope—gave people a sense of ownership in the project. The "Ideal Theater," should we have the good fortune to actually construct it, would be the realization of the best ideas of many people.

The process might also, I hoped, avoid throwing us into a situation like the one in Indiana. It would be my job to safeguard our theater's art throughout what would be an arduous, voraciously time-consuming project, and I needed to be able to rely not only on staff loyalty, but also on staff understanding and, as much as possible, their appreciation of the process. It was a daunting prospect.

Well, were we going to attempt to build a new facility? The architects had determined that we would benefit greatly by such a course, and had identified three huge old electric power plant buildings located virtually next door to the Performing Arts Center, on the Milwaukee River, as the best potential site.

In 1974, Charles McCallum, the retiring MRT managing director whom I was replacing, took me to the old East Wells Street Power Plant and asked me to stand on tiptoe and look through the window. I gasped. There was a *huge* room in there with a clear span of seventy feet to the ceiling! Charlie said, "Someday the Rep will have a theater here." Now the architects had verified Charlie's instincts, but how in the name of heaven were we to pull it off? I've never felt smaller in my life than standing gazing at those immense piles of brick.

But forward motion had been established. An early version of the *Theater Facilities Impact Study* had been printed up and the MRT board president, Joyce Broan, and I began quietly distributing it to various powerful individuals in the community, accompanied by an admonition not to panic: the Rep wasn't going to leap off a cliff in the next five minutes, but this *did* describe our serious needs . . . etc., etc. I particularly remember a visit that Joyce and I made to Sol Burstein at Wisconsin Electric Power Company (WEPCO). Sol was greatly interested in the community and, though nearing retirement, listened with great care to our story and promised to pass on our materials. Sol retired before all the big things happened, and his name never came up among those who were involved, but I suspect that without his generous ear on that day I wouldn't be putting all this down on paper.

Views of main turbine room.

The Germ of an Idea

At about this time, Joyce Broan, Sherrill Myers, Bob Beckley and I attended an urban design conference in Pittsburgh, sponsored by the National Endowment for the Arts and Partners for Livable Places, and entitled "The Arts Edge." The major theme of the meeting was an emerging concept of public/private partnership which reported successful cooperations between nonprofit arts organizations and commercial developers and detailed the positive financial fallout for the nonprofits. Richard Weinstein, who had been involved in the legendary sale of air rights by the Museum of Modern Art in New York to a commercial real estate developer, was particularly eloquent on the prospects for the sale of air rights and sale/leaseback structures.

Our group returned home fired with enthusiasm. And at this point, fortune once more smiled upon the Milwaukee Rep. T. Michael Bolger was just coming on as board president. A lawyer with the firm of Quarles & Brady, Mike was a visionary of the highest order. He not only embraced our ideas about some sort of commercial involvement, he rapidly perceived possibilities for the entire block which the East Wells Power Plant shared with the 19th-century Pabst Theater and a surface parking lot for the Pabst and City Hall employees. Edison Street ran north and south through the parcel, but if it were closed, the block as a whole could be made available for a mixed-use development.

Even as we tried to figure out how the Rep could best approach the problem of the acquisition of the Wells Street Power Plant, other activities continued. Sherrill Myers assigned a graduate class of architects at the University of Wisconsin-Milwaukee the task of designing a hypothetical new home for the Rep on the block in question. Money was to be no object; it would be a new structure. But they were to meet extensively with the Rep to determine needs and also research such things as power lines, zoning laws and parking needs in the area.

In late November of 1982, Wisconsin Electric announced that it was closing down the power plant and putting it on the market. Mike went into high gear, in an urgent search to make contact with a developer who might talk to us. I then had one of those accidental but pivotal conversations which you long remember because they set an entire process in motion. I was serving on the board of the Milwaukee Artists Foundation, an organization which focuses on the needs of the smaller arts organizations in town, and one evening after a board meeting I stood on the rainy, chilly steps of Lincoln High School, which had been converted to a center for the arts. With me stood Bill Randall, executive vice-president of First Bank Milwaukee, and Kevin O'Connor, alderman for the downtown district in which the power plant was located. They were quite excited about our concept for a new life for the old buildings and Bill said, "Don't let Mike do anything before he talks to me."

That same night I went to a showing of the models and drawings that Sherrill's class had prepared for a "new home" for the Rep. Mike was there, of course. I remember being concerned that I was leaving for Japan the next day and that this was my only chance to get his attention and extract his promise to call Bill before he did anything further. He promised he'd do so.

I flew off to Japan to make advance arrangements for the tour we were to make the following spring, and when I returned ten days later, my desk was a sea of pink message slips, each one saying: "Call Mike Bolger!"

I did call and the news was terrific, beyond my wildest hopes. Bill Randall had brought Mike and Sherrill Myers together with Steve Dragos, executive vice-president of the Milwaukee Redevelopment Corporation. The MRC, as it is called, had recently brought to a triumphant conclusion a long-drawn-out and difficult

Early study model.

project, the $77 million downtown retail development known as "The Grand Avenue." A nonprofit organization backed by major Milwaukee corporations, the MRC encourages and assists development in downtown Milwaukee.

The timing was perfect: the MRC, flushed with success, was raring to go. They had development expertise and credibility far beyond anything the Rep could hope for. In addition, they had a new president, Fred Stratton, Jr., chairman and CEO of Briggs & Stratton Corporation. Fred was also, in his quiet way, a visionary who was willing to spend time and energy on a real long shot. It is appropriate to let him speak for himself here:

> Mike Bolger came to see me about the Milwaukee Repertory Theater's desire to turn the soon-to-be-abandoned Wells Street Power Plant into a new home for the Rep. I was aware that the plant soon would be empty and that a number of not-for-profit organizations coveted it. I thought Mike's concept was superior, because it included not just a home for his organization but a two-square-block commercial development as well. While MRC offered development expertise, Mike was more interested in the credibility MRC could provide. I thought the concept had about a one-in-twenty chance of success, but if successful, it would be terrific, and, not wanting to rain on Mike's parade, I agreed to help.

A real measure of Fred's attitude also shows up in the cover note he wrote to me when delivering his written comments: "As I think it over, I could have spent more time on the universal skepticism we faced in the early going. In fact, that skepticism was a strong motivation to me to get the job done."

And skepticism there certainly was. Nevertheless, the Milwaukee Repertory Theater and Milwaukee Redevelopment Corporation formed a joint venture for the purpose of exploring the idea. The next step was to get an option on the power plant to hold it off the market while we pursued our planning. Mike Bolger, Fred Stratton, Steve Dragos and I paid a call on Charles McNeer, chairman of Wisconsin Electric Power Company. Thanks to Mike's eloquence, Fred's strong support and Mr. McNeer's own great concern that the old plant be the focus of a project with genuine benefit to the community, the MRT-MRC joint venture was not required to purchase an option, but was given a six-month period during which WEPCO would keep the power plant off the market to see what we could come up with by way of concrete plans.

14

And so things heated up and the round of breakfast and lunch meetings became endless, day after day. At this point, the project became multilayered, with many tracks running simultaneously. These tracks continued right to the end, and could be described as community involvement, economic feasibility for the development as a whole, architectural design and budget for the MRT portion, financing of the total project, and operating projections for the MRT once it occupied its new home.

Mike Bolger and Fred Stratton became the co-chairs of a volunteer task force and were able to bring major community players into its membership. Two subsidiary working committees were also formed: the lawyers committee and the bankers committee.

In the meantime, the Milwaukee Rep was committing its own money to an assessment of its prospects. Richard Weinstein was brought in to describe the shape of the Museum of Modern Art deal and its ramifications for different situations. The fund-raising firm of Brakeley, John Price Jones was hired to do a fund-raising feasibility study. Marketing research was done via MRT staff visits to Actors Theatre of Louisville, the Cincinnati Playhouse in the Park and Indiana Repertory Theatre. The marketing director of Arena Stage, Washington, D.C., was brought in to consult on single-ticket marketing strategies, something which the heretofore heavily subscribed MRT would have to develop in a new home with a radically increased seating capacity.

At this point, the Department of City Development (DCD) joined the team and allocated $30,000 to the Milwaukee Rep to commission two important feasibility studies. A local economic research firm, The Rooney Group, was asked to study the economic feasibility of the site. Beckley/Myers was commissioned to do an urban site plan for the total area, and to suggest a design which could integrate the existing power plant structures and the Pabst Theater with new commercial spaces. Their design, which furnished the prime organizing principle for the project, received an award from *Progressive Architecture*, and the Rooney Group reported that the area could generate enough income to make it financially viable.

During this period, weekly—and sometimes twice-weekly—meetings were taking place at the Milwaukee Redevelopment Corporation's offices in the basement level of the Grand Avenue, where representatives of the Rooney Group, the MRC, Beckley/Myers, the DCD, the MRT and Morse/Diesel struggled with physical design concepts for the project and an endless series of approaches to financing it.

Morse/Diesel, a nationally prominent construction and construction-management firm which had built the Grand Avenue, was keenly interested in being considered for this project, should it ever get off the ground. To position themselves, and to help the Rep, their local vice president, Robert Schulz, offered the services of Morse/Diesel to work with Beckley/Myers to develop cost projections for the MRT's proposed conversion of two power plant buildings into new quarters. They would do this at no cost, provided they were given the job, if and when. After consulting with the MRC about Morse/Diesel's performance on the Grand Avenue, the Rep accepted the offer.

It was during this period that two individuals began demonstrating the great and beneficial impact they would have on the project: Frank Krejci and Richard Rogers.

Frank Krejci, at that time a member of the management staff at Briggs & Stratton, was treasurer of the Milwaukee Redevelopment Corporation. Frank has training and expertise in real estate development, acquisitions and mergers, and venture capital programs. Through the generosity of Briggs & Stratton, he was able to spend enormous amounts of time working through a whole series of financing packages which were explored. He insisted that the Rep had to be better off at the end of the process than when it began and exhibited endless patience and inventiveness in trying program after program.

Richard Rogers became technical production supervisor at the MRT at a moment when he could make major contributions above and beyond managing well the Rep's production department. With a degree in civil engineering, depth of background in technical theater and, again, a large capacity for work and the endless detail spewed out by the enormous construction project, he and his department became key to the design and installation of proper equipment for the new theater and a real resource to both architects and construction management during the building process.

The project was slowly moving from the "Great idea, Mike. Crazy, but great!" to the "Great idea. Will it work?" stage, and in the process was picking up spin and drawing in a wider and wider spectrum of people of skill, as well as power, within the community.

This was the time when I learned to ask. Always ask, no matter how stupid you may fear the question to be. Always ask. You have no other way to keep up with the real estate lawyers, financial wizards, city development experts and commercial developers. I learned, as fast as I could, whole new areas of financing and real estate law that I will, hopefully, never need to know again, but desperately needed to know *then*. It takes stamina, patience, willingness to read *all* the print, fine or otherwise, and to insist that jargon be explained in plain English.

It's out of this era that the phrase emerged that I still hear kiddingly applied, "Hey, honey, how're your soft costs?" A young hotshot from the Rooney Group was rattling off all the various ways in which costs and financing might be juggled to make the project feasible. Among the terms being tossed around was "soft costs." I kept asking what they were, and seemed to get one anwer one minute and a different answer the next. Finally I all but shouted, "Stop! This may be stupid, but you've *got* to tell me precisely what soft costs are, since I have a sneaking suspicion that I'm going to have to pay them!" Soft costs, it turned out, included about $250,000 of legal and accounting fees, insurance, bank fees, licenses and filing fees. After the meeting, my assistant at that time, Lisa James, whispered in my ear, "Don't you feel a bit like Little Red Riding Hood going through the forest, when a big furry creature steps into your path and says, 'Hey, honey, don't mind me, I'm just a *soft* cost!'"

It is difficult to capture the degree of effort and determination exhibited by the core group of people at this time. I will always remain a bit astonished and humbled by the level of time which people committed to the project. And while it is certainly true that many had something direct to gain, many gave generously of time and skills to bring something into being which they perceived as good for Milwaukee.

And Mike Bolger was everywhere, selling, doing it with mirrors and smoke, exuding enthusiasm and optimism, soothing ruffled egos, insisting. In short, he was a true believer. And without a true believer, a project like ours may never have come to completion.

While all this planning and financing activity was going on, the board of the Milwaukee Repertory Theater made the first of several courageous choices. They authorized the contracting of Beckley/Myers to complete designs for the conversion of the power plant buildings to our use and, specifically, to draw up specs for the massive job of interior demolition required to clean out the immense boilers and turbines. This was done with the knowledge that it was a gamble: if the project did not proceed, we would be out by as much as $250,000. And yet, if it did go ahead we *had* to be ready to move.

From Speculation to Commitment

The design for the Ideal Theater now moved out of the speculative phase, off the wall of the green room and onto drawing boards which had to deal with the spatial realities of a turn-of-the-century power plant. The challenges this posed are best described by Sherrill himself in his portion of this book. I'd just like to point out that this is where we began to reap the benefits of all those early discussions which so clearly defined the basic principles of spatial organization we wanted to see followed in an Ideal Theater. While the construction-paper theater in the green room had been nearly round, and approximately two stories high, we were preparing to occupy two five-story rectangular industrial buildings with two-foot-thick brick walls and which, while they shared a common wall, did not have matching floor levels. Had we begun without all those intensive early meetings, I believe that both the Rep itself and the architects might have been driven by the givens of the building, rather than forcing those givens to respond to very clearly articulated needs. In a conversion of an existing structure, there will always be compromise between the abstract ideal and the preexisting conditions, but I believe that the arduous look we took at space needs without reference to any existing building strengthened our ability to deal creatively with those massive structures sitting there on the Milwaukee River.

Beckley/Myers' open design process continued throughout this period, with many members of our company walking the two blocks from the Performing Arts Center to their office overlooking our hoped-for home. They sought input on every segment of our operations and feedback on designs as they emerged. Our master carpenter consulted on the catwalk and rigging system, as did two lighting designers who often work with us. John Dillon, the artistic director, participated in every step of the design for the larger theater's playing area, giving us the two vom entrances to the stage which are such an improvement over the single down-center entrance in the old theater. A house manager had a suggestion about audience flow which eventuated in the design that joins the orchestra and balcony lobbies into an open promenade.

The process was open to everyone, but no one was required to participate. It was clear, however, that those who couldn't be bothered were reducing their right to grumble about things which might get overlooked in their areas.

I want to be clear about something: Beckley/Myers designed the building. We did not, although we often feel as though we did, so well does it respond to our

Programming workshop in old PAC green room.

expressed desires. Beckley/Myers' staff and our staff hammered out many solutions together, yet it was the architects who kept in mind the overall structural and esthetic integrity of these facilities. They successfully carried through on their philosophy by creating a whole which satisfied their client's desires and at the same time has a life and an architectural personality which is their own. (Perhaps one of the happiest circumstances in the project was that their esthetic and ours coincided so well.)

All this design activity was predicated on the presence of a commercial developer who would take on a large risk and an intensely complicated project. Here the Department of City Development lent a hand. Jon L. Wellhoefer was the DCD's prime participant in the project at this time. (He later moved to the private sector to become executive vice president of the Milwaukee Redevelopment Corporation.) As Jon recalls it:

> I remember the breakfast meeting when the joint venture just began to make developer contacts. I had just returned from Dallas and knew that the Trammell Crow Company was active in the development of an Arts

District in that city. It was at this meeting that I suggested we talk with Jon Hammes. Hammes and I had worked together on the Park Place project.

Jon Hammes was at that time head of the Trammell Crow Company's Wisconsin operation. Originally from Racine, he had a strong commitment to his home region and a dedication to high quality in the projects he handled. Perhaps only Jon could have as sympathetically embraced the "City Hall problem," about which more later.

Mike Bolger met with Jon Hammes and they liked one another immediately. But let's let Mike speak for himself:

> I was able to have breakfast with Jon Hammes shortly thereafter, and I found him willing to become an enthusiastic participant in the project. We had slowly put the pieces together to make the project work. That is, we now had the joint venture with the Milwaukee Redevelopment Corporation, which is the development arm of the Greater Milwaukee Committee, the main group of Milwaukee's "movers and shakers." We had the power company ready to deed the property to us if we could show it that we could make it happen. We had a respected developer with financial clout, construction acumen and sensitivity to the Rep's needs in the Trammell Crow Company. We also had the commitment from the city of Milwaukee and its Department of City Development to help us with the infrastructure for the project, and a committed theater board in place to complete the project.

Let's turn now to a few other fronts upon which negotiations were proceeding. This middle term of the project's life was a veritable thicket of obstructions to be overcome and avenues to be hotly pursued, only to be discarded when they proved to be blind alleys.

"The City Hall problem." This had two manifestations, one architectural and one human. The architectural problem was City Hall itself. Built in 1895, it is a wonderful Flemish Renaissance building with two graceful towers. The copper-clad towers and ornamental facade of City Hall are treasured downtown landmarks. Would the new development and its office tower overshadow its venerable neighbor across the street? Would the traditional view of City Hall as one traveled east on Kilbourn Avenue be blocked off? Perhaps even worse, would the architectural style of the office tower, hotel, etc., clash with the 19th-century styles of City Hall, the Pabst Theater and the East Wells Power Plant? Jon Hammes and Trammell Crow embraced

Trammell Crow tower to the right, with subsequently built office towers illustrating the "Milwaukee feel."

Sketch of proposed theater with City Hall in the background.

the problem rather than avoiding it. A series of meetings occurred during which we demonstrated through photos and drawings that the office tower would be nicely framed by City Hall's twin towers as one proceeded up Kilbourn. Jon hired the Houston firm of Skidmore, Owings, Merrill to design the Trammell Crow portion of the development and they attacked the problem in a straightforward manner.

Adopting Beckley/Myers' basic plan of organization, with the office tower, hotel, Rep facilities and Pabst Theater holding down the corners of the development and facing inward to a grand rotunda, Skidmore, Owings, Merrill developed a design for a brick-and-masonry tower with multiple facets which, while certainly modern, related very well to its neighbors. In consequence, Milwaukee Center, as the development was finally named, has a real "Milwaukee feel" to it, unlike a few other of the glass-and-steel office towers scattered about the city. It may be accidental, but I would hazard a guess not, that the two office towers since constructed nearby also reflect this hard-to-describe, but very definite, "Milwaukee feel."

The other City Hall problem was human and carried greater potential for disaster. It was the mayor of Milwaukee himself. Henry Maier was concluding a term of office of record-breaking length at this time. He had, over the years, created a clean, well-run city government and was dedicated to the city's best interests—as he saw them. Now, however, as he neared retirement, there was little incentive for him to embrace a high-risk project. If problems developed, the mayor would be faced with leaving office on a sour note, and leaving the problems with his successor. Yet, without the mayor's wholehearted support, the project would simply not go forward.

This is where real thanks are owed to Mike Bolger and Jon Hammes. They reached the mayor, won his support and managed to keep his faith and friendship intact over a long, stormy period, when lesser men might have lacked the patience or skill.

Another thorny problem we faced was community acceptance of the project's potential benefits versus its probable cost. Early on, Mike and I had to face the executive committee of the United Performing Arts Fund (UPAF). This organization runs an annual multi-million-dollar campaign which provides, in effect, the Milwaukee Repertory Theater's sole local private-sector operating support. (For the 1991-92 season we received, for example, $742,000 from UPAF.)

The arts fund struggles constantly with the issue of outside fund-raising within the community by its member groups. There is a legitimate fear that heavy capital, endowment or debt-reduction campaigns may, unless properly handled, impair the fund's massive annual campaign for operating support. But the fact that UPAF, while it works on behalf of the MRT, isn't actually the MRT greatly magnified a problem which would have existed even if we were doing all our own development work. A rock upon which many a theater company has stubbed a toe is the manner in which a successful capital campaign may wreak havoc with the following, or concurrent, year's operating campaign.

So the MRT had to negotiate with UPAF. These negotiations continued from the earliest days through the opening of the theater. They consumed large amounts of time and complicated many things, but it was absolutely crucial that the fund's operating campaigns be unharmed.

Because of the arts fund, from the first the only approach we felt could be considered was one which required little or no broad-based fund-raising. How could that be possible? Mike Bolger pinned his hopes on a sale/leaseback scheme, the essence of which was that a nonprofit corporation sells its property to a commercial developer who is able to receive certain tax benefits, such as historic tax credits, facade donations and low-interest bond financing. At the end of the conversion, the non-profit leases back its property. It was the hot thing in real estate development and nonprofit/commercial partnerships at the time.

Mike's enthusiasm could be overwhelming. I remember sitting at an Arts Fund executive committee meeting as he described how we were going to build a glorious new theater, spawn a mixed-use development and "it wouldn't cost the community a dime." My heart sank as I stared out the window at the huge power plant structures across the way, and I made haste to correct him and say that of course *some* money would have to be raised, but that our goal was to make it minimal. (I would live to be glad I'd uttered those words, when some were accusing us of hoodwinking the community.)

And it was genuinely our intent. Frankly, at the beginning we couldn't see how we could just go out and raise the necessary funds in direct solicitation. And wouldn't it be grand to pull off a wonderful financing scheme?

So we tried—and failed. During this period we—meaning the group as a whole, including the City of Milwaukee—tried a whole series of possibilities. It seems pointless to describe them in detail here, since none of them ever came to pass, but we should give them at least a passing glance, if only to get a sense of the time and thought being expended seeking an answer.

Sale/leaseback! This much-touted mechanism of the early '80s was supposedly destined to open up new vistas of the promised land for nonprofit arts organizations. Except that those early to the trough had been shockingly piggy. (I seem to remember an instance cited of a New England college that had sold and leased back the majority of its campus.) So Congress was in the process of passing new legislation which would remove nonprofits firmly from the picture.

Except for those projects already underway. So the Rep mounted a fierce and highly directed campaign to prove that we were sufficiently underway to qualify. Letters, calls, documentation, trips to Washington. Finally, thanks to Senator Bob Kasten (R) and Congressman Jim Moody (D), with help from only recently retired Congressman Henry Reuss, the Milwaukee Repertory Theater was grandfathered under the new tax legislation.

Yet despite all that, the general market for sale/leaseback deals began to go sour,

Historic interior of power plant.

the profit margin available to commercial investors became discouraging, and we could find no one interested. Trammell Crow negotiated with us for a seemingly endless period of time but we could never reach agreeable terms. So the financing mechanism that we'd first perceived as an ace turned out to be a joker.

What to do? The city of Milwaukee stepped in and tried to help, by applying to the Federal Governement not once, but twice, for an Urban Development Action Grant. But UDAGs were being phased out and in these final rounds the money went to cities perceived to be the most economically distressed. Milwaukee, though a slowly recovering "Rust Belt" city, was no match in urban decay for New York, Detroit or Newark. Goodbye UDAG hopes.

25

Then there were historic preservation credits. If the power plant could be placed on the National Register of Historic Places, we could structure a deal to use the historic tax credits and a donation of the historic facade to our financial advantage. If you've never applied to place a building on the Historic Register, let me tell you, it's *some* process! Intensive documentation is required, and although the southernmost two power plant buildings, built in 1890 and 1900, were handome enough, they certainly had not revolutionized the architecture of their day. But a process developed within those power plants *had*. It was in these buildings, and, with their boilers, that two WEPCO engineers, John Anderson and Fred Dornbrook, demonstrated that if coal were pulverized and dropped from above into the boilers, and the coal dust was ignited as it fell, it burned with greater intensity and efficiency than ever before. This pulverized coal process had revolutionized the production of electricity in the United States. *This* was worth placing on the National Register of Historic Places!

After producing reams of documentation, we were informed that our building qualified. (You can see the plaque on the building today.)

But that was only the first step. In order for the project to qualify for tax credits, the National Park Service had to approve our plans to convert the now historic structure. Right. And we'd forgotten that we were planning to remove the smokestack to make room for a backstage area. Furthermore, we didn't know that the Park Service claims jurisdiction over the design of any new buildings contiguous with historic buildings.

The regional Park Service in Denver rejected our plans, and we made a formal appeal to the office in Washington. Sherrill, our lawyers and I boarded a plane, armed with documents and arguments. We made our pitch, were listened to judiciously, and told our conversion plans could be approved only if we retained the smokestack and got rid of the office tower. "But," said the adjudicator, "do invite me to your opening."

As each one of these fancy mechanisms faded away over the horizon, our potential fund drive grew proportionately. From zero to $4 million, to $6.5 million, to $8.5 million . . .

But it's time to backtrack a bit now and talk about how we went beyond the wishing stage and actually *got* the building we were struggling to finance. Charles McNeer, in a move that exhibited great vision and good tax sense, deeded the land and buildings along the river to the MRT/MRC joint venture on January 4, 1984 for the sum of $1.00. The magnanimity of the gift was astonishing, but equally important was a provision of the deed which stipulated that at least 35% of the land *must* be used for a theater. This meant that those grand old buildings were firmly in our hands and destined for one purpose, and one purpose only. And since the north-ernmost building was basically just an eight-story shell around an enormous boiler system, and therefore unusable, the land on which it sat could be made available to Trammell Crow, at a price.

Wisconsin Electric Power Company had empowered the joint venture and, ultimately, the Milwaukee Rep, to play with the big boys. Henceforth, we owned 50% of the land in the project, and the city of Milwaukee owned the other half. This meant

Original power plant.

Conversion in progress.

that we had real power to enforce the intention of the other partners, as expressed by William Drew, then commissioner of city development: "If it doesn't work for the Rep, it doesn't go."

This is as good a time as any for a little discussion of power. The MRT and Beckley/Myers had developed a deeply cherished view of what our facilities *ought* to be and how they ought to figure in the development as a whole. We now had to fight to see that our goals were met. And we had to understand that goodwill alone is not sufficient. Power is not being beholden. It was critical that the theater company be perceived as contributing as much to the community as it was receiving from the power structure. It is all too easy for a nonprofit arts organization to find itself the pawn in various economic development strategies. What WEPCO had done was to make the Milwaukee Repertory Theater a player to be reckoned with.

Their faith in us, as exhibited by that grand gift, had to be justified. One way to do that was to step firmly up to the table, not just to protect the Rep's flanks, but to work with our new partners, Trammell Crow and the Department of City Development, to create a development in which everyone would win. We were constructing a system on that block which resembled a balanced aquarium. Not only would we share common walls and common access, but we were assuming that together we would keep that parcel of land active from early in the morning until late at night. The businesses in the office tower would draw people into the area during the day; in the evening the theaters would light up and a new cycle would begin. This activity, dubbed by Frank Krejci counter cyclical traffic, was a major component of our concept.

This premise, as well as Trammell Crow's determination to build in the downtown area, offered a solution to one of our greatest headaches: parking. Though there were a number of lots and structures within three blocks of the site, there was nothing deemed adequate to the demands of the project. No parking, no theater. No parking, no office tower. Our planning group originally began by eyeing nearby properties, only to run head-on into a group with whom we should have been best friends, given our plans to preserve the old power plant. But Milwaukee's historic preservationists quite rightly took a very dim view of any attack on the old buildings running south along the west side of Water Street. Several heated and inconclusive meetings ensued, at which we were forced into a role we'd seldom played—the guys in the black hats.

So Trammell Crow's announcement that they were willing to undergo the mammoth expense (nearly twice the cost of above-ground parking) and the problems of installing a four-floor, 800-car parking structure *beneath* the development came as a saving grace. And a daring move. None of the other developers with whom we had held discussions had been willing to consider going *down* into a site directly adjacent to the Milwaukee River, one certain to contain the debris of a century and a half of old Milwaukee. But if our concept was correct, that underground parking structure could be assured of occupancy both day and night.

As we met steadily and design conference followed design conference, the basic shape of the project grew clearer and clearer and we turned to wrestling with *who* would be responsible for *what*, not only financially, but in the long term. Areas of responsibility were negotiated.

And here the vision and determination of the city of Milwaukee came into play. The city would assume the financing burden for all public areas and concourses, as well as partial financing of the parking structure, a portion of which was to be available to city employees. To do this, a Tax Incremental Financing (TIF) district would be delineated. Tax incremental financing is a means by which a city can finance public portions of a project by advancing the money and using the *new* taxes generated by the development over and above the land's unimproved valuation to pay off this advance. Essentially, new tax revenues are diverted into repayment. Once the TIF loan is paid off, the city's general revenues will benefit. Tax incremental financing has been a classic form of municipal assistance to new development, but it requires very skillful estimating on the part of the city's financial experts. For days, the question was: could the number of dollars the city could safely risk on a TIF district match up properly with the level of financing required?

In the meantime, I was struggling with another form of financial projection. If we got our wish and occupied new quarters which would more than *double* our square footage, would the building bury us? Furthermore, would increasing the scope of our operation from two to three performing spaces by adding a cabaret necessitate staff expansion that would throw our operating budget into the bends?

I budgeted and rebudgeted. We actually put together a hypothetical but minutely detailed operating budget for a first season. I was obsessed with worry about costs of operating the plant. Budgeting theatrical costs was something I knew how to do. But the utilities, maintenance and janitorial costs of almost 145,000 square feet? I asked my friends at companies who owned and operated their own theaters to send me audits, so I could see if there was a consistent percentage of budget for facilities costs, adjusted for the facility's square footage. The answer was not really, though some similarities turned up. I also asked questions and received astute advice on how to watch for the peak periods which the utilities company will use to set your rates. I listened with dismay to the news that a huge rotunda of a lobby and the uninsulated stretches of converted old building had created skyrocketing utilities bills at another theater.

And I sought advice from Wisconsin Electric itself. With great patience their consultants began with square-foot cost projections and revised them again and again to take into account our pattern of electricity usage, including the big draw when those stage lights fire up. The architects' mechanical engineering consultants, Ring & DuChateau, not only worked on designing the heating system, they advised me on the cost of city steam.

It was somewhere during this that I had a classic nightmare. In my dream, I was in my office in the new theater. (I had pored over the plans to such an extent that my dream greatly resembled today's reality.) My office had (has) a glass wall and when a sudden hush fell over the outer office, I looked out to see what was happening. One by one, every member of the staff was silently rising and making for the exit. What, I wondered, could be wrong? Then I saw a small, neat little man in a business suit approaching. He entered my office, saying, "Mrs. O'Connor, I have your first month's electrical bill," and placed an *enormous* piece of paper on my desk which said $250,000!

I was also facing the small matter of fear, personal fear. The pressure was on. At one breakfast meeting at the University Club where Mike and I were seeking the support of half a dozen influential men from the business community, one of them turned to me and said, "I need an anwer to one question. If we do this, will you stay?" Meaning, not jump ship, no matter what. Live to eat the fruit of the tree I was planting. I said yes, and I'm still here because I took the question seriously.

Fear—of failure, of losing one's position within the pecking order in the business community, of what the media will say, of losing one's job—fear is the wild card in a project of this size. The danger is real and coolheadedness very nearly your only resource. And, to speak frankly, the pressures are greatest on those who've elected to take on leadership positions in the community and to *act* on their vision. This is why I shall be eternally grateful to Mike Bolger, Jon Hammes, Fred Stratton, Charles McNeer, Bill Drew and Jon Welhoeffer. Many others as well, of course, but these men accepted real public exposure.

All of our work on operating projections made it clear that the new theater would be a new financial ball game for us, and that we must not put ourselves in a position where financial stress threatened our freedom of artistic creativity. I kept reminding our board that getting the building built was the beginning, not the end, of the process and that I estimated it might take as much as five years of operation in our new home for us to learn the best way to handle it.

The Rep had at that time a board-designated cash reserve, some of which was being drawn down to make payments to the architects. Our estimates showed the Rep's operating budget jumping by about $500,000 in the first year in the new building and growing steadily thereafter. To help build reserves adequate to buffer any problems in this area, we went through the demanding process of applying for a Challenge Grant from the National Endowment for the Arts. This $200,000 grant, matched 3 to l, would add $800,000 to our existing reserves and give us both working capital and a hedge against disaster.

Beckley/Myers had progressed greatly toward the final design of the theater, which Morse/Diesel was projecting at a cost of roughly $11 million, and Trammell Crow was proceeding to arrange commercial loans for their portion of the project. Yet no viable financial engine had as yet been devised to carry the Rep into the construction of a new home.

However, by this time powerful forces in the community and city government were convinced that the "theater district," as the media had dubbed the project, would indeed be an asset to Milwaukee. And so the city stepped forward to offer something which we had previously discarded as being out of the question for a nonprofit arts organization like the Rep: a bond issue by the Redevelopment Authority of the City of Milwaukee (RACM). True, the bond issue would be a loan, not a gift, but it would be a loan at a reasonable rate of interest and would give us a big chunk of the cash required to start construction.

This was the moment I realized that Mike's indefatigable efforts to convince the community had succeeded. We were on our way to converting a power plant into a theater—and there was no backing out. From a long period of driving the project, we were entering a period when it would drive us.

The Ride Begins

We had already had a taste of things to come. The transfer of the old power plant structures to the MRT/MRC joint venture occurred in the dead of a Milwaukee winter. Two days later, with the mercury congealed at -15° F, my telephone rang. It was Mike James, of Wisconsin Electric. It was he who had been in charge of the old plants and been so helpful in taking us through them, explaining their contents, digging out old records, etc. Mike said, with just the merest trace of glee in his voice, "I'm sorry to bother you, Sara, but the sump pumps in your power plant are frozen."

Our power plant! On with the boots, the gloves, the muffler, to tramp across the street, descend to the basement of the hulk to stand with Mike staring at silent, dead pumps, discuss the options and authorize the expenditures (of *our* money) necessary to get things going again so we could keep the Milwaukee River at bay.

It must be noted that Wisconsin Electric was extremely helpful during this period and we were able to transfer without a hitch services for security, assume insurance liability, and know they would always be available to answer questions about their old plant. And of course, there was Wil-Kil, to keep the river rats out of the building.

On May 22, 1985, the official groundbreaking took place, preceded by a big luncheon at which both Mayor Maier and Trammell Crow himself spoke. The ceremony itself was simultaneously silly and moving. Silly because it took place on the parking lot at the northeast corner of the project (now occupied by the Wyndham Hotel). You can't break ground on an asphalt parking lot, so a truckload of dirt had been provided, with the mayor's assurance that this was city of Milwaukee dirt, not suburban soil masquerading under false colors. About a dozen of us who were intimately connected to the project stood in a circle around the edges of the mound, and on command, thrust our chromium-plated shovels into the dirt and tossed it into the air, whence it of course fell directly back into place.

It was moving because nearly every speaker, including me, had something to say about the importance of art to the life of the city. It was also, on a personal level I don't often examine, interesting to discover that I was the only woman standing in that circle. In fact, while numerous women played a part in the story, especially those on the MRT board, I can think of only four who were out on the firing line on a daily basis: myself, Connie Gavin, Donna Meyer and Gina Spang. However, our roles were varied enough so that perhaps it's fair to say that our sex held its own.

There is a picture of Mike Bolger and me at the groundbreaking, grinning like fools. Every picture of me after that until October of 1987, when I put on a long dress, is in a hard hat. For we were now underway, and I was on the site daily.

As mentioned earlier, we had primarily used ourselves as consultants on the project. One early brush with a theater consultant had been unsatisfactory—all we seemed to get were generalities when we were seeking specifics. But now the architects were approaching the most ticklish point of all, the design of the configuration and

Power plant's auxiliary generator.

Top floor battery room, which will become office space.

spatial relationship of the stage and house in the mainstage theater. Beckley/Myers were facing formidable demands. We wished to increase our seating capacity from 504 to at least 700. We wished to flatten the curve of the audience address to the stage. (The Todd Wehr theater in the Performing Arts Center has an almost square stage.) We wanted good acoustics. We insisted that the old theater's feeling of intimacy be retained, despite the increased number of seats. We wanted it to be strictly functional and to reflect its site in the power plant, but it shouldn't be too cold. Intimacy was fine, but we needed a proper angle of throw for the lighting instruments and room for an adequate catwalk system. And on and on and on . . .

Sherrill and his team listened, absorbed and worked. They actually got to the point of building a model of the auditorium. Sherrill then approached me with a request that showed the full degree of their commitment to excellence. With no hint of "architect's ego" he explained that they'd reached an area where they felt they needed the added experience of a theatre consultant with intimate working knowledge of what such spaces required. At that moment my trust in Beckley/Myers was confirmed.

Remembering our one less-than-happy experience, I began questioning my friends in the field. From the West Coast, one name came up again and again: Richard Hay. He had designed the Angus Bowmer Theatre at the Oregon Shakespeare Festival and the new Old Globe Theatre in San Diego. He is a much respected, highly creative scene designer. After a talk with Tom Hall, managing director of the Old Globe, I got in touch with Richard Hay. Would he be willing to spend a few days working with our architects to find approaches to the design of a space which would work for us? Richard was a bit hesitant. He had designed theaters, but never before served as a hit-and-run consultant, so to speak. But at last he agreed to spend a weekend with the architects. Artistic Director John Dillon was to be involved as well.

They met, talked, worked furiously with intense concentration, and parted after the weekend with a sense of mutual respect. What emerged from the process was: a space with a catwalk high enough to be useful, low enough to provide a sense of finitude to the volume of space; a large, but not hypnotically high opening between the stage and the thrust; a backstage area big enough to hold two complete sets on wagons; a balcony that thrusts forward into box loges as it approaches the proscenium wall, thus further closing in the space; a fine steel-mesh screen behind the last row of seats which acts like a scrim, allowing latecomers to see the stage, yet wrapping around the seating area. The pitch of seats is sufficient, but not too great. And there are three inches more legroom between rows than in the old theater. The basic playing area is not raised. John resisted Richard's desire to raise it, and while we do often now build it up, it is useful to be able to begin at ground zero, as it were.

While all this was going on, another drama was assuming some urgency. The bond issue was to occur in late summer or early fall. (We were now in 1985.) This was of particular importance, since it was the architects' plan to remeasure, and redraw accordingly, once the interior demolition was complete and the buildings had been opened up to reveal secrets and flaws that no amount of structural testing and boring could uncover. If too much time elapsed, this would not be possible and construction would have to take place on a fast-track, adjust-as-best-you-can basis. This would create undefined, but quite possibly large, additions to cost.

The city of Milwaukee was using the Milwaukee office of the Minneapolis-based firm of Miller and Schroeder to work out the details of the bond issue. The calculations needed to be precise. We were trying to identify a bond issue which would give us the money needed to bridge the period of a capital campaign and its extended pledge payments, provide the best relationship between interest earnings on the money from the capital campaign and payments of interest on the bond issue itself, yet keep the issue as small as possible because it was, after all, a loan which would have to be paid off.

Frank Krejci took on the considerable responsibility of overseeing the creation of this financial mechanism, and a series of meetings organized by Jon Wellhoefer (who had recently made his move from the Department of City Development) began at the offices of the Milwaukee Redevelopment Corporation.

Also underway was another piece of the puzzle—arrangements for the transfer of the north parcel of land from the MRT/MRC joint venture to Trammell Crow.

And at this point two other people assumed prominence in the story. Active for some time, they now entered the heart of the whirlwind. At the time WEPCO deeded the land to the joint venture, the hard-working lawyers committee disbanded and unanimously recommended that Larry Jost, a partner of Mike Bolger's at the law firm of Quarles & Brady and the firm's representative to the volunteer committee, should now be formally retained by the Rep, especially as Foley & Lardner represented Trammell Crow. Thus, when it came time to square off, the real estate experts of the city's two largest law firms would face one another.

A word here about legal representation. The costs of appropriate legal support were part of our budget, and it is the best money we ever spent. The Milwaukee Repertory Theater owes a debt of gratitude to Larry Jost and Connie Gavin, another real estate lawyer for Quarles & Brady, for the fact that it rests so securely in the ownership of its new home. I owe them personal thanks for the fact that, despite the pressures and conflicts, they remained in good humor and made the process always clear, understandable and intensely interesting.

I did learn, however, that I couldn't just shift responsibility to the lawyers and tell them to call me. To help them steer me in the right direction, I had to read, question and, ultimately, understand all the fine print so I knew as clearly as they where the important issues lay. And only the owner can stand firm. They could advise the owner, but the owner had to choose to fight or give in. Certainly they clearly understood what was in the best interests of the Rep and fought with endless patience on our behalf.

Surprisingly enough, this is also where my experience as managing director of a

Section drawing through Powerhouse Theater.

nonprofit theater company was valuable. First, in terms of process, all those years of labor negotiations as a member of the negotiating committee of the League of Resident Theatres had brought me under the tutelage of Morris Kaplan and Harry Weintraub, LORT's counsel. They had taught me that a misplaced or omitted comma can change the entire interpretation of a sentence and that you ignore the fine print at your peril.

Second, there is a world of difference between the nonprofit corporation which operates with *no* margin or, one might even say, *below* margins, and a profit-making corporation designed to protect or improve existing margins. I've been given to believe that, as this project progressed, I gradually acquired a reputation as a tough negotiator. As best I can discover, in the profit-making world this "toughness" can be a personal trait. In truth, I'm not particularly tough, nor do I enjoy battles. (Well, maybe a *little* bit.) But back in about 1959 I made the harebrained decision to cast my lot with the world of the nonprofit theater. Beginning each year with a big gap to fill between income and expenses makes it clear that you are standing, on behalf of your institution, on a *very* narrow ledge with your back to a thousand-foot drop. This creates a tendency to plant the feet *very* firmly and stiffen the backbone. Often, when people were inclined to believe that I *wouldn't* move, the truth was that I *couldn't*. I had zip for maneuvering room and a fragile institution to protect.

At this point, there were two forms of negotiation going on, the first involving primarily Mike Bolger, Jon Hammes, Fran Brzezinski and myself. This was the transfer of the north parcel of land to Trammell Crow. The amount of money it would generate for the Rep was a critical element in our financial program. Mike and Jon had several conversations about it, to none of which Fran or I were a party. But it was up to Brzezinski and O'Connor to hash out the deal. This was the first of many negotiations with Fran, the second-in-command in the Milwaukee office of Trammell Crow, and who would eventually shoulder the full burden of their end of the project. I found him to be a tough negotiator who would try anything on for size, who had intelligence, stubbornness and patience, but who was straightforward and pleasant to deal with.

Now, Mike was certain that Jon had agreed to $4,250,000 as the price of transfer. Jon was not certain of this at all, and it appeared to me that Fran had marching orders not to exceed $4 million, a sum more than the probable market value of the land alone, which also contained a building expensive to demolish. The city of Milwaukee cleared the way by agreeing to take on the expense of the demolition via a turnkey contract with the Rep to do so. A firm from Chicago was contracted by Morse/Diesel at below the amount authorized by the city, and the wrecking ball began to swing.

And Fran and I haggled. In classic fashion, he started low and I started high. It was clear to me that we'd not get $4.25 million, but I had to get more than $4 million. Back and forth we went, until we stuck at $4,060,000, and to break the deadlock I went down to $4,055,000. I suppose I should have felt defeated that we didn't get what Mike wanted, but I knew that $4 million would work for our financial projections. Still, it always makes me laugh when someone asks me why Trammell Crow gave the Rep such an esoteric sum for the land, knowing it was just the result of a couple of negotiators trying each other on for size.

This situation did bring to the fore the sole advantage which a nonprofit corporation could bring to the mix. The land was sold for $3,055,000, a figure closer to its true market value, and Trammell Crow made a $1,000,000 tax-deductible contribution to the MRT, in recognition of the MRT's part in conceiving the project. In turn, this generous gift is recognized on the south portal of the Milwaukee Center. One enters the MRT portion of the project through an arch which says "Trammell Crow Pavilion."

At the urging of Larry and his team at Quarles & Brady, seconded by the architects, a second fierce contest was underway. We insisted that before any land transfer could take place, a remarkably detailed Agreement of Easements absolutely had to be negotiated. We felt that without such a comprehensive working out of access rights, responsibilities for repair, pathways for utilities, etc., before Trammell Crow and its lenders took over, the Rep could find itself badly crippled in the future. Our ability to work out appropriately protective terms for the Rep would be radically reduced once we relinquished ownership of the land. Ergo the intense negotiations in which Larry and Connie pressed the Foley & Lardner team hard to get a fully executed Agreement of Easements—a legal document which would act as a life preserver for us just three years later.

Meanwhile, back at the ranch—the bond issue ranch, that is—very little was happening. Miller and Schroeder would bring in a proposed strategy for a bond issue, and when it didn't fulfill our requirements, they would return to the drawing board, not to be seen again for two or three weeks. September came and went. October came and went. And still another problem began looming over the horizon. New federal legislation concerning municipal tax-exempt bonds would take effect January l, 1986, and it was thus imperative that this issue be signed, sealed and delivered before that date.

Not to mention the steadily constricting construction calendar. In order to disrupt MRT audiences as little as possible, we had to open at the beginning of a season or not until the following year. And our sights were set on the fall of 1987.

Time slipped steadily away and the frustration mounted just as steadily. The apparent deadlock *had* to be broken. This was accomplished by enlisting the services of Robert W. Baird & Co., a Milwaukee-based investment firm, first to advise, and then to take on the problem themselves. This was an unusual step, and the day representatives of the two firms were asked to sit down together was roughly as memorable as putting two tigers in a cage together and asking them to solve a crossword puzzle.

The matter ultimately rested with Baird alone, and time was now rushing toward the deadline. They pulled out all the stops and Steve Kent, a young member of the firm, began to put together a model for a bond issue, working furiously against time.

The board of the Milwaukee Repertory Theater was now faced with a momentous decision. They had exhibited considerable courage up to this point and had backed Mike Bolger solidly. By the same token, he had up to this point personally led the way and assured them that the Rep was not yet in too deep to get out. Now, however, a vote to proceed with the bond issue would mean the die was irrevocably cast. And the Rep would not only be building a new theater, it would be assuming a several-million-dollar debt for the bond issue and accepting the task of raising millions in a capital campaign.

Mike liked to use metaphors to describe the way the process felt. He'd describe what he and I were doing as paddling a canoe upstream or slogging through a swamp. Well, if we made the next step it would take us onto a raft headed for white water, and no one could as yet discern if that faint roar in the distance was a crowd at the finish line or falls we'd be swept over.

On the afternoon that the board was to make its decision, the computers were spitting out analysis after analysis as Steve Kent and Frank Krejci struggled to appropriately size the bond issue. As the minutes ticked by and I realized that Frank was actually pacing the floor, the thought crossed my mind that we resembled a scene in a cheap novel about the business world. Finally, six million seemed to be the right number when plugged into Frank's scenario, a written explanation of how it would all work was prepared, and Frank and I dashed to the board meeting.

Nerves were taut. Everyone wanted to do it, but no one wanted to inadvertently scuttle the Rep. One Board member articulated what everyone was wondering by asking if the Rep carried directors' and officers' liability insurance. The answer was no, but perhaps it would be prudent to get some for the duration of the building project.

It was a long, thorough meeting. At its conclusion, the vote was "yes," and on December 31, 1985, the president and secretary of the Milwaukee Repertory Theater signed 27 separate documents prepared by an exhausted group of lawyers representing Trammell Crow, the city of Milwaukee and the MRT. These documents accomplished a complex series of land transfers: from the joint venture into the hands of the Redevelopment Authority of the City of Milwaukee, which was issuing the bonds, then back to the joint venture, which dissolved, and ceded the land to the MRT, which upon verification of a wire transfer of $4,055,000, transferred the north parcel to Trammell Crow. This is, of course, a simplified picture, since the City and Trammell Crow, along with its two subsidiary corporations, were entering into a complex agreement governing their collaboration in the construction and responsibility for the public and commercial sections of the "theater district" soon to be officially known as "Milwaukee Center."

Getting it Together and Paid For

Work now commenced in earnest. The Chicago construction firm had experienced delays in demolishing the north building which they claimed were due to the discovery of "unexpected asbestos" in the structure. A close reading of the construction contract made it clear that it was their responsibility to examine and assess the premises carefully prior to signing the contract which designated their fee. Nevertheless, they put in a claim for a considerable overage.

It was a different story in the two southern buildings destined to become our new quarters. Here HSA Contractors, specialists in asbestos removal, well armed with Wisconsin Electric's meticulous records of PCB contaminants remaining in the buildings, completed on time and under budget a scrupulous removal of every vestige of asbestos and other problematic materials. Still, it was costly. When someone asks if we had an asbestos problem with the building, my stock reply is, "Not unless you consider a quarter of a million dollars a problem."

So, as the winter wore on, we had a leveled site to the north and a couple of buildings ready for interior demolition.

Demolition! I had seen it from afar, seen the wrecking ball taking down buildings. I had not, however, really contemplated the hellish complexity of interior demolition. And now the demolition contractor was attempting to dismantle two-story boilers. Generators weighing many tons and whose copper blades had to be cut out, blade by blade. Conveyor belts that moved hoppers of pulverized coal to be dropped into two-story boilers encased in inches of brick. Miles of huge piping. Rows of gauges and knife switches mounted on banks of marble slabs. Iron staircases, two-foot-thick walls. And all this to be done *inside* the shell of the building, in a hell of roaring noise, thick clouds of dust, arcing welding torches. I would go inside and watch in awe as a man hung in a bosun's chair 40 feet off the floor and laboriously cut out huge chunks of steel and attached them to a crane to be lowered. Yes, a huge crane sat for months *inside* what was to become the Powerhouse Theater.

The smokestack which had apparently been our main claim to fame on the

Left, *Area destined to become rehearsal halls.*

Below, *Powerhouse Theater under construction.*

View of construction from above.

National Register of Historic Places was constructed of double rings of brick surrounded by a layer of concrete and had to be dismantled by hand, ring by ring, by a group of hardy men wielding jackhammers hundreds of feet in the air in the high wind. The debris was simply dropped inside, falling with a resounding crash to a huge pile growing in a corner of the building once occupied by a boiler.

It's obvious that the masses of demolition debris had to go out to be trucked away, but one price we paid for the delay (remember the bond issue?) was that our buildings weren't cleared out before Trammell Crow began excavating immediately next door for their four-level underground parking deck. So now there was a huge hole confronting the eastern doorstep which we'd intended to use for hauling away debris. (It also turned out that floor had to be strengthened to hold the trucks.) The final solution was to cut a huge opening in the northwest face of the building and get our stuff out as fast as possible before excavation began for the office-tower foundation next door. Once that began, we'd be ringed on two-and-a-half sides by the river and holes in the ground.

Morse/Diesel was, of course, acting as our construction manager. Meticulously detailed contracts had been drawn up by Quarles & Brady for both Morse/Diesel and Beckley/Myers. We had incorporated Bob Schulz's budget of $11.5 million in the contract. Morse/Diesel was to manage the project for us and bring it in on budget. They would report directly to a building committee of the board, but we would be spared the killing weight of managing the project for ourselves; they, in return, would receive a six-figure fee.

The project team consisted at first of Jim Barron as project manager and Glenn Penkwitz as job supervisor. Glenn fought World War III from a construction trailer parked on Wells Street next to the site. Building new buildings is one thing; tearing apart old ones is another. The project made Glenn crazy. He was nonetheless doing a terrific job, though I was never sure that it made him happy to have a crazy woman as the owner's rep, especially one who kept going off to Japan. Glenn's last experience of Japan was going in with the American troops at the end of World War II.

Then one day Glenn was gone. I was told that he'd taken early retirement at 63. Whatever, I missed him. And how he came to be replaced made me uneasy. The lack of numbers of personnel adequate to the size of the job would play a big role in the scenario of a major crisis which would arise at the end of the project. More about that later.

Once the building was open, some of our fears were confirmed. The north wall, though apparently 18-24 inches thick, was in reality thin masonry walls encasing rubble fill, and the interior tile was bowing out under the weight of the fill. We considered replacing the wall, but since the major structural elements were sound, the final solution was to pin it together with massive structural bolts.

During this period, two new efforts began, one offensive and one defensive. The proactive effort was the beginning of a campaign to raise $10.6 million (including $600,000 as a match for the NEA Challenge Grant). Brakely, John Price Jones, who had done the initial feasibility study, was hired as campaign consultant. Ike Hancock came to Milwaukee as staff representative.

The first challenge was campaign leadership. Ike was insistent that it had to be top—and topnotch—corporate leaders. Fred Stratton, who had cochaired the task force, and John (Jack) Murray, CEO of Universal Foods, seemed good partners. Fortunately, Fred was already deeply committed and Jack was willing to come on board for the first-ever multi-million-dollar campaign to be attempted by the Milwaukee

Repertory Theater. The $10.6 million was a big goal for this town, especially with only about an 18-month time frame. You will note that certain of those involved in the first task force rolled on to get the job done.

To reach a goal of that magnitude, a large lead gift was required. A lot of hair-tearing and fingernail-biting went into figuring out where to find it. And lightning struck again, in the form of the sale of the Allen-Bradley Company to Rockwell International, pouring millions in assets into what had been a small corporate foundation to create the Lynde and Harry Bradley Foundation, one of the nation's largest.

Mike Bolger described what happened:

> It became evident to me during the course of this project that what makes something like this work is the ability to attract the people in the community who can make decisions and influence large sums of money, by getting them to share in the vision of the project. For example, when it came time to begin the fund drive, it was important that the Bradley Foundation be one of the lead gifts in the community. Since I had no influence at the Bradley Foundation, nor did anyone else on the Rep board, it became important to find somebody who did. Fortunately, we were able to get John Kelly, president of Park State Bank, who was a good friend of I. A. Rader, the president of the Bradley Foundation, to persuade him to give the Rep its lead gift. Mr. Rader called me from San Diego after John Kelly had talked to him and told me that because John had asked him, he was going to commit $2 million as the initial gift to the Rep fund drive.

This seems to be the appropriate spot for a word about timing. While to some extent you are yourself part of the timing and you can do much to keep events flowing in the direction you desire, you must nevertheless be in sync with the mood, the aspirations, the direction being pursued by your entire community. If you are, you will ride the tide. If not, you may find the tide is out when you want to launch your boat. Our project first rode the crest of community pride at the successful opening of the Grand Avenue, the big downtown retail mall. The project then became the centerpiece of the focus on downtown revitalization which was current policy for both the Milwaukee Redevelopment Corporation and the Department of City Development. Milwaukee was also a city with a long history of love and support for the arts.

It was logical for Milwaukee to perceive a theater company as an anchor for a mixed-use development.

Furthermore, this project could not have happened in the '70s as the city struggled to surmount a rust-belt recession. Nor would it be probable amid the economic uncertainties of the '90s. It was clearly a by-product of the optimistic '80s. That's not to say that nothing can be accomplished now; I merely wish to note that the scenario would in all probability be quite different.

I mentioned a page or two back that two efforts were underway. The defensive and reactive program was an effort to stave off a challenge in the state legislature to our request for an exemption from property tax on our new facility. The Performing Arts Center is county-owned and therefore exempt, but nonprofit organizations are not automatically exempt from property taxes in Wisconsin. If the MRT had to pay property taxes on the old power plant, the drain on our budget would put us under within a year or two.

We made our proposal based on three premises: 1) Wisconsin Electric, as a public utility, paid relatively low taxes that went to the state, not the city, so our move would not change anything on the local public tax rolls; 2) the MRT had not paid property taxes in the PAC, so nothing would change there either; 3) the MRT had been instrumental in the creation of a huge downtown development whose commercial components would eventually throw off thousands in property taxes, yet the only way we could survive as the nonprofit component of the development was to be tax-exempt.

Things looked good until two members of the state Assembly hit the papers with an attack on the Rep, implying that we were trying to take away existing tax revenues and that we were supported only by the rich and elite, who should bloody well provide the money. One of the Assembly members suggested that the Rep was a place just for the mink-coat crowd, which prompted a female state senator from our district who was supporting us to sashay into the legislature in a mink coat. But what made the comedy less than amusing was that the Assembly person was herself a subscriber and knew better, knew that our audience includes many of modest incomes.

Curiously, of the many rough things that happened over the time it took to complete the project, it is this episode which I remember most painfully. For whatever purpose, maybe simply to get media attention to appeal to what they perceived to be their constituency, two politicians tried to make a mockery of our most basic purpose, which is to make our art accessible to as many as possible. One reason for increasing our seating capacity was to be able to maintain inexpensive seats. In the fifth year in our new theater, we still have $6.00 seats available, with a dollar off for students and senior citizens. We believe that the arts feed the human soul and are not a plaything for the rich.

Ultimately, the property-tax exemption went through and a year or so later a general exemption was passed for performing arts centers.

In the spring of '86, the demolition firm from Chicago finally got around to filing suit for its claimed extra expense for asbestos removal. While we felt they didn't have a leg to stand on, the affair dragged on for many months until a settlement was reached which was still well within the original sum authorized by the city.

With a projected opening just eighteen months away, both construction and the capital campaign went into high gear. And yet again, fortune smiled on the MRT. (This is getting boring, isn't it?) Donna Meyer succeeded Mike Bolger as president. Donna is perhaps one of the nicest people of all time and, as it developed, one of the most indefatigable fund-raisers. She would ask the devil for money and make him glad he gave. With Mike Bolger, Fred Stratton and Jack Murray continuing to go after the big fish, Donna became almost singlehandedly the backbone of the campaign. She organized and encouraged scores of volunteers, working voluntarily full-time with a staff assistant, out of campaign headquarters in donated office space. The professional fund-raiser who had so carefully plotted out the campaign proved less effective on a day-to-day basis, and the contract with Brakely, John Price Jones was terminated.

The capital-campaign cabinet met almost weekly, strategized and carried through. It was a laborious process, because every single approach to a potential corporate or major individual giver had to be coordinated with the United Performing Arts Fund, to make sure it didn't harm their campaign for our operating funds. Donna and I had seemingly endless meetings with UPAF, yet somehow we made steady progress. The capital-campaign cochairs pledged generous leadership gifts which spurred our progress. Because of the UPAF campaign, ours was not to be a broad-based appeal, but rather a highly focused one. Only the seat campaign, to come at the very end, would be opened up to our whole subscription audience.

The building committee of the MRT board, first chaired by Mike Bolger and later by Allen Rieselbach, of Reinhart, Boerner, Van Deuren, Norris & Rieselbach, was also shouldering its considerable task of approving trade contracts and monitoring the progress of construction, as reported by Morse/Diesel. Al Rieselbach had been a member of the original volunteer lawyers committee and now, as a member of the

MRT board, he was making his considerable knowledge of the legal end of construction available to the cause.

Meantime, old Mother Nature was flexing her muscles. The summer of 1986 brought record high water to the Great Lakes region. Assorted ecological predictions began appearing in the press suggesting that this was merely the beginning of a cycle which would create flood-level conditions in the near future. And guess who'd just acquired an old power plant whose foundations stretched down into the Milwaukee River, whose level is controlled by the level of Lake Michigan?

Pools of water began rising in the basement of our building, inhibiting construction, necessitating the installation of emergency sump pumps and creating general consternation. It was determined that the floor of the old plant would need to be raised, but this was possible only to a degree which would not inhibit our need for basement storage space (such storage space needing to be, in a Catch-22, *dry*). It finally became clear that flood control necessitated the construction of a dock wall along the river edge of the building. This was, of course, an unanticipated expenditure.

And coordination continued with Trammell Crow, including an astonishingly emotional wrangle over the MRT's decision to put a copper roof over its lobby space, instead of the glass roof planned for the Trammell Crow rotunda, arboretum and galleria. The whole thing was an object lesson in what can happen when you think people have been fully informed, and they haven't. It left me with a strong propensity to verify for myself whether or not information has been transmitted.

The "Copper Roof Wars" came about roughly as follows: When the decision for all glass enclosures had been reached, the MRT was contemplating a lobby design which was basically a glass-enclosed addition to the face of the old building. As we attempted to accommodate the demands of the Park Service vis-a-vis the Register of Historic Places, this design altered to a raised lobby allowing public access beneath it to the development at large and giving access to the 720-seat theater across bridges into two of the old plant's massive original window embrasures.

This was terrific for giving access to the development and allowing it to have a grand archway at each of the three major entrances. But any spatial change creates corresponding spatial alterations. We now had a lobby with a roof lower than previously expected. To keep our spectators from sizzling in a glass greenhouse would mean significantly increased costs and hundreds of feet of air-conditioning ductwork which would in any case destroy the interior beauty of the glass roof.

We could *not* afford either the cost of initial installation or the ongoing increase in cooling and heating costs. So Beckley/Myers turned to a copper roof, with the idea that it would blend in well with the neighboring Pabst Theater and City Hall. So far, so good; but somehow no one had told Trammell Crow's Jon Hammes. We each assumed someone else had relayed the information, most probably through Trammell Crow's architects.

Jon was furious when he found out. His deep loyalty to the design integrity of his portion of the project made him deeply resistant to changes to any part of the project unless he felt he had been sufficiently involved. We, on the other hand, felt bound by our own constraints and needs, and I became mulishly stubborn on the subject of our right to do as we pleased with our part of the project. For whatever reason, we locked horns and the Copper Roof Wars were on.

I can remember a meeting with Fran Brzezinski in the Trammell Crow offices, where we gazed down upon a scale model of the project. Fran pointed out the architectural integrity of a total system of glass roofs and I replied, somewhat rudely, that only someone in a helicopter would care. (This is not, strictly speaking, true, since the upper floors of the office tower overlook the rest of the development.)

Meantime, Bob Schulz, of Morse/Diesel, who was working on both projects, advised a cooling-off period as the budgeting for Trammell Crow's portion of the project proceeded. And when all was said and done, and if you visit the Milwaukee Center today, you will find that the rotunda and the arboretum have copper roofs and only the two galleria arms have glass roofs. Like all hot, but minor, skirmishes, the Copper Roof Wars disappeared into the history of the project and Jon and I remain cordial friends.

However, a more important controversy arose at this time, and one whose outcome was to have a lasting—and positive—effect on the development. This was the Riverwalk.

Back in the very first planning stages, there'd been talk of a Riverwalk. The idea of a system of walks bordering the Milwaukee River throughout the downtown area, as a way of making a plus out of the fact that the river cuts directly through downtown, had been championed by Charles McNeer and embraced by the Greater Milwaukee Committee. And, indeed, it was a good idea, if not critically important to our project. During the early stages, when we were carefully marking the plans with indications of who was responsible for what, the Department of City Development had accepted responsibility for the Riverwalk "as a low priority."

Now, many months later, the city was committed to the maximum for Tax Incremental Financing for a project whose costs were rising. An attempt by the

Department of City Development to get an appropriation from the city's General Fund failed and the Riverwalk became a hot potato. The DCD fervently desired to pass it on to the Rep, on whose property it would, after all, abut. Charlie McNeer insisted that Mike Bolger and Fred Stratton had promised him a Riverwalk as part of the Rep project. This was entirely possible, but news to me, and watching the probable rising costs for my own project, I dug in my heels and insisted that the last I'd heard, the city was paying for any Riverwalk.

Impasse. Both McNeer and the DCD wanted the Rep to pay for the Riverwalk and I wouldn't do it. It was going to cost roughly $400,000 and we didn't have it. This was one time when I'm glad I drew the line and refused to give folks the easy way out, for the result of my refusal was that the DCD went to the state of Wisconsin for a grant of $125,000, matched by $125,000 from the city, and rounded out with $150,000 from the MRT. And our flood-control dock wall became the base for a handsome

View of new facilities from Wells Street bridge.

Riverwalk connecting the Wells Street bridge with the Kilbourn Avenue bridge. It added a goodly sum of money to our construction budget, but this past June, when I watched the crowds gathering for a crafts fair, and whenever I see the brave row of Milwaukee-style harp lamps reflected in the river, I am very glad we were finally cornered into making this addition to downtown life. Thanks should be extended here to Mike Wizniewski, of the DCD, who fought so hard to get us the state money.

Now is the moment to go back to my early concerns about Morse/Diesel's staffing of the MRT project. When Glenn Penkwitz left at the height of the demolition phase, the first word I had was that Morse/Diesel would simply have someone from the neighboring Trammell Crow project pick up the slack. This was fine for a few days, but I wrote a formal request to Morse/Diesel for a new on-site job supervisor, as any fool could see that the project was too big to be handled part-time.

To my relief, within a week or so Gina Spang had been hired and was on the site. Gina is an exceptionally bright young engineer who had at this point just graduated from Marquette University. She plunged in with a will and began straightening out the numerous snarls. Nevertheless, despite her talent, this was her first major job and she lacked the experience to successfully muscle the contractors on the job. Gina's inexperience, combined with the downright horrifying complexity of converting a power plant to a theater plant, made it necessary for Jim Barron, the project manager, to leave the office and spend the bulk of his time on the site. Without Jim's indefatigable supervision and Gina's attention to detail, I seriously doubt that the theater would have opened on time, but the fact remains that the project was very seriously understaffed. The situation was aggravated when Jim was also assigned to a project at the Medical College of Wisconsin and became stretched hopelessly thin between the two. Hindsight makes this easy to see, but even at the time I was uneasy. Yet assurances came readily from Morse/Diesel that everything was under control. It wasn't, but they were, after all, the "experts" at construction management and this was my first experience.

Make no mistake about it. We were undertaking a once-in-a-lifetime project. There'd been nothing before it to set a precedent, and it was infinitely more complicated than constructing a new building. But Morse/Diesel's policy of consistently understaffing was at best penny-wise and pound-foolish, and at worst, downright negligent. As construction managers, they were, by and large, calling the shots and should have adequately met this responsibility.

And the day of reckoning was fast approaching. The MRT had set its sights on opening in September 1987. Trammell Crow's portion was due to open in August

1987, and the early speculation on the street was that the MRT, an arts organization inexperienced in construction, would never make its deadline.

The summer of 1987 was a major test of nerve. The labor contracts for the majority of the construction trades were up for negotiation that spring, and by July the ironworkers, plumbers and electricians were on strike. Some contractors were totally stalled, others falling steadily behind. The labor dispute was between unions and contractors, but it was the Milwaukee Repertory Theater that was being squeezed.

So we looked at the options, none of them encouraging. We could open the season in the Pabst Theater, which I estimated could cost us an extra $200,000-$250,000. Our subscribers, whose numbers had swelled by an extra 2,300 (to 20,800) in the heat of excitement, weren't too keen on seeing productions in the Pabst, unless it was *A Christmas Carol*. As an alternative, we could push the opening back to October and run the season out into June, also not ideal. And the push to get open, even in October, would cost an unspecified, but large, amount of overtime as the trades struggled to meet our deadlines.

Nevertheless, I felt it would be better in the long run to get open in our new home, even if in a still-unfinished state. So that's what we did. There will never be a way to know if it was the right decision. I may have been driven by the need to at last get the damn thing over with, but I still feel glad we did it.

And here we learned a big difference between the theater and normal practice in the construction industry. In the theater, our deadlines are real, absolute and un-avoidable. We must open on the day we set. In the construction industry, deadlines appear to function more as general goals; hence, the norm is that projects go well past their scheduled opening dates. Imagine the shock to the contractors when they discovered we *meant it*!

To their credit, most of them rose to the challenge. And Jim Barron was everywhere, problem solving, heckling, pleading, threatening. One day I heard him thunder into the phone: "Dammit, we've got an opening to make!" and I realized that he'd caught our fever.

Overtime flowed, as dry wallers, electricians, plumbers and ironworkers fought to finish under the wire. The ironworkers installed the balcony safety rail not once, but twice, in order to provide better sightlines. And then grinned amiably when I brought beer the next day to thank them for their patience.

I must put in a plug here for the quality of the skilled labor found in Milwaukee, and the dedication of the contractors. It wasn't true in every case, of course. We had a very bad time with a dry-wall contractor who apparently ignored specs deliberately in order to cut his own costs. Nevertheless, I remember with pleasure the surprise expressed by Colortran when they came in from California to install our new light board. Expecting the usual difficulties, they were astonished when the installation went as smoothly as a hand slipping into a glove. The Milwaukee electrical contractor had properly prepared the hundreds of electrical connections.

The conversion of the East Wells Power Plant into a new home for the Milwaukee Repertory Theater reminded me forcibly of an obvious fact I think we are prone to overlook: buildings are built by *people*. They don't spring into the air straight from the architects' plans. Every square of masonry, every foot of concrete, every length of pipe, every pane of glass, every electrical connection is put into place by human hands or by a piece of machinery guided by human hands. In certain areas, the skill required is breathtaking. The Milwaukee Rep's new home is a tribute to those who conceived, designed and financed it, but also to those who *built* it.

As the push went on at the Rep, things next door in the Trammell Crow project were falling further and further behind. I must admit that this was something which had never crossed my mind as a possibility. Something, I suppose, about the difference between big and small, commercial and not-for-profit. At any rate, it was with considerable misgiving that I learned their finish date was moving back by months, even as Fran Brzezinski and I continued our endless negotiations over the shared costs for the south portal and the electrical vault on the east side of our building.

But we were going *in*. On Labor Day weekend, 1987, the MRT administrative staff climbed the stairs to take possession of the fifth floor, still unfinished and deep in construction dust. The switchboard was installed in the totally unfinished reception area and our dauntless receptionist began virtually camping out in an area occasionally shared with a homeless person or two.

The City Building Department, none too happy with our presence in a building still under active construction, laid down the dictum that hard hats were to be worn *anywhere* outside the administrative area. So it was clear to your co-workers as you donned your hard hat that you were making a trip to the one functioning restroom in the building.

The Rep company performed with extraordinary patience under stress. The first rehearsals for *The Matchmaker* took place on the stage of the neighboring Pabst Theater as we waited for permission to occupy a rehearsal hall. The box-office staff functioned out of cardboard boxes. The stage carpenters moved into their shop while construction carpenters were still finishing the backstage area next door. This created one of the more absurd exchanges of that period, when a construction carpenter asked one of our stage carpenters when he'd be finished in that room—he'd been there forever—only to be informed by our carpenter that he worked there and was building scenery, not the building!

This was also the epoch of the raccoon. The scenic artist came in one morning to find small paw prints leading straight across an enormous drop he was painting. One of the construction workers insisted that it was a raccoon, an idea we scoffed at until the MRT's chief operating engineer trapped him and escorted him with ceremony to a wooded suburb. This urban and cultured raccoon has since become something of a legend at the MRT. (One of his compatriots was later also encouraged to cease his theatergoing habit.)

The opening was approaching, and the building was receiving its first uses in its new character: a big fund-raiser, and then a special party, sponsored by Wisconsin Electric, a celebration for all those who had in some way had a hand in bringing the dream to fruition. We labored carefully to create a list for that event which would be truly inclusive. It's hard to describe the elation and gratitude I felt when I stepped onto our new stage to introduce Mayor Maier, Mike Bolger, Charles McNeer and Fred Stratton to a group of more than 600 Milwaukeeans who had believed enough in a crazy dream to give time, money and expertise to it. And the entertainment that night was provided by the MRT company, not a visiting star.

I was specially pleased to have a chance to thank the construction workers on television and startled to receive their thanks next day. They'd been watching. We got a temporary occupancy permit one hour before the first preview and three days later *The Matchmaker* opened in our 720-seat theater on October 25, 1987, but that big glorious comedy wasn't the end of the story. We still had two more theaters to finish, a $10.6 million campaign to complete, construction to close out—and, unbeknownst to ourselves, we were steering straight for an iceberg.

Thanks to the superb efforts of Donna Meyer, Fred Stratton, Jack Murray, Mike Bolger and scores of others, the fund campaign was moving toward its goal. Naming gifts of $750,000 each from the Milwaukee Foundation and the Stackner Family Foundation allowed us to name the 200-seat black-box stage the Stiemke Theater, in honor of Walter and Olive Stiemke, and to christen the small restaurant/bar and 116-seat cabaret space the Stackner Cabaret. Wisconsin Electric's topping-out gift allowed them to choose the wonderfully apt name of the 720-seat theater: the Powerhouse Theater.

The Seasons of Our Discontent

The winter of 1987-88 could be best named "the winter of our discontent." We'd passed third base, but were most definitely not yet home free. Our audiences, confused and daunted by the as-yet-unfinished character of Trammell Crow's Milwaukee Center and the lack of finished decor in our own theater, grew increasingly disgruntled as they struggled into the theater through plywood passageways.

On one horrifying below-zero December morning, our janitorial staff found the lobby three inches deep with water. A pipe had frozen in an area intended to eventually be in the interior of the Milwaukee Center, yet currently only an open-air construction site. Our sprinkler system had been triggered. With commendable speed they got industrial water-removing vacuums and the show went on that night. But it was a cold, grim winter.

In March, the Stiemke Theater and Stackner Cabaret opened their doors on their first performances, and the Building Committee of the MRT, who had put in long hours throughout the construction period, prepared to close out construction and lay down their burden.

But unfortunately the time had not yet come. For months, the monthly computer printout of costs submitted by Morse/Diesel had indicated a manageable $200,000 in cost overrun. As each month's report came, I scanned it for further overages, but it remained stable. Each time a contract was let, Morse/Diesel gave a report on how things were generally balancing out. Tired and harried, we accepted the prognosis of our construction management.

In truth, I should have known we were in deep trouble, and probably would have known if I'd been handling the construction budget myself: difficulties with demolition; high water; the delay in the bond issue, which left no time for the architects to redraft and forced the project onto a fast track; the state's insistence that we fireproof all the exposed old iron trusses, the labor stoppage in the summer of 1987—all these things added up to an indeterminate, but large, cost overrun.

But I wasn't handling the construction myself and certainly wasn't qualified to do so. I had my hands full just being a responsible owner's representative, negotiating with Trammell Crow, lending support to the fund campaign, and, of course, running an active theater company which continued producing throughout the life of the project, including two overseas tours. So I was grateful that we'd hired

Morse/Diesel to handle that end of things, even though their services were costing six figures.

I suppose, too, that we all *wanted* to believe them. To believe that we'd pitched a perfect ballgame, beating out all the normal odds by getting exactly the facilities we desired without the cost overruns which plague most projects. We (or at least I) should have seen the warning signs, but we accepted Morse/Diesel's assurances in docile relief.

Then came a somewhat desperate call from Jim Barron, indicating to me that he felt the project had gotten away from him in the last horrifying weeks and that the cost overrun might be closer to $500,000 than $200,000. I was concerned, but not panic stricken, and instructed him to get together all the pertinent documentation so that I could break the bad news to the building committee in a sensible fashion.

I didn't pick up the phone and immediately inform my board president and the chairman of the building committee. This was the biggest error I could have made, one that was, in hindsight, nearly fatal. I had grown too accustomed to shouldering immense burdens and overcoming obstacles on my own, without unduly frightening the troops. But the president and the building committee would share with me the brunt of what was to come and the phone call should have been made.

But it wasn't made, and I settled into an uneasy period of waiting for Jim to come up with the facts and figures, a period which stretched to over five weeks, during which time a building committee meeting came and went without any formal warning signals from Morse/Diesel.

At the same time, I was beginning an attempt to peer into the future to try and determine if our carefully constructed financial machine was working. Its delicate balances between construction and bond payments and cash in-flow from pledge payments from the bond drive were theoretical, a computer model. The question was: how well was this standing up to reality?

I will be the first to confess that I have no training in making complex financial projections which take into account accumulated interest and the time-weighted value of money. (We are fortunate to now have a controller with excellent skill in these areas.) However, I figured I could at least take a comparative look at the schedule of bond payments and the scheduled pledge payments. Each time I ran these figures, we came up short, to the tune of something like two million dollars. Even clumsy attempts to throw in interest didn't help. In a panic, I began to wonder if our theoretical engine had failed us.

56

The next day there was a meeting at the Morse/Diesel offices of Bob Schulz, Sherrill Myers, building Committee Chairman Al Rieselbach and myself (Jim Barron had by now given up on Morse/Diesel to join another firm). The purpose was to prepare for a building committee meeting late the following afternoon. The discussion went smoothly, and as the meeting broke, Bob Schulz handed me a manila envelope. Throughout the construction process, I had been signing purchase orders and looking at bids, so I thought nothing of it. It was late, and I didn't open the envelope until the following morning. When I did, the bottom fell out. I knew where the missing millions had gone. The envelope contained, along with a note asking me to "sign and return," a whole stack of change orders for work which I knew had long since been carried out. My first thought was, "How stupid does Bob think I am?" I had been on the job site daily, closely following the sequence of construction. These change orders should have been submitted months and months ago, and many of them were large enough to have necessitated discussion by the building committee. My second thought was that this was an attempt to get my signature and thereby shift onto my shoulders a certain amount of blame for the coming debacle.

It took me about an hour and a half to recover from blind panic and an urge to leap from my window into the Milwaukee River. This time I sat down and wrote a letter to Frank Krejci, now our board president, and Al Rieselbach, and called to warn them that it was coming. The situation was dire, but we had, if push came to shove, reserves adequate to pay our bills. This would leave us operating with nothing behind us, but not carrying long-term debt.

The sense of betrayal was overwhelming. The members of the building committee in particular, and the entire MRT board in general, were deeply angry at Morse/Diesel. They had raised 10.6 million dollars from the community, and declared the campaign a success, on the assumption that we were not running too far ahead of budget. The prospect for public embarrassment was hard to face.

The first cry was to sue Morse/Diesel. But we were still in the closeout period and Al Rieselbach was able to remind the committee of the painful reality that we probably could not successfully accomplish closeout without Morse/Diesel (although the possibility of going to another firm for closeout was seriously explored). Frank Krejci felt strongly that the first thing needed—and needed desperately—was to determine the exact amount of the cost overrun. Only after we'd pinpointed the problem could we make decisions.

This proved easier to say than to accomplish. Morse/Diesel simply didn't know, nor could they readily determine the cost—something nearly unbelievable on the part of what had been recommended to us as a capable construction management firm. But we began to dig.

At the end of that season, Peggy Rose, the MRT's fine business manager, resigned after twenty-four years of exceptionally capable service, to pursue new avenues in her life. We were fortunate to be able to fill her shoes, and then some, with Leslie Fillingham, a young woman who is a CPA, extremely skilled at computer applications to accounting and financial projections, and with a flexible and questioning mind. One of the first things she confronted was the hideous problem of Morse/Diesel's flawed records.

In the first instance, their computer program was terribly ineffective, and for what should have been an obvious reason. Such a program should automatically bump forward all changes in budget, in estimates, in final payments, etc., into a change in the final projection for that line item. Morse/Diesel's did not. The final cost projections were left to be adjusted manually by the project staff. This meant that as the project, bitterly understaffed, roared to its conclusion, the on-site project manager became increasingly overburdened and less and less capable of also handling the paperwork involved in these computations. Thus, the Morse/Diesel accounting department not only did not supply the project manager with correct final cost projections, but allowed the printouts to show grotesqueries like an already made payment that was higher than the final projection. This seems to me to be a fatal lack of backup for the project manager.

The building committee and I had, of course, been seeing these computer projections on a monthly basis. I, in particular, should have picked up these oddities. The only thing I can offer in defense of my own oversight is that I viewed my responsibility as relating primarily to verifying the contracts, purchase orders and invoices which were the raw data being fed into the computer, and which were the basis for our borrower's requisitions to pay the construction draws. We are so dazzled by our machines that it never crossed my mind to question the computer program or to look at more than the bottom line. After all, we'd hired construction management. Live and learn.

It took a full year to complete the closeout, and it was a brutal process, walking a tightrope over the fiery trough of possible public embarrassment at the cost overrun, coupled with an equally dangerous weakening of the MRT's painfully established financial credibility in the community if we dragged out too long the payments to contractors. To be fair, I should say that our project had finally acquired Morse/Diesel's full attention, and Bob Schulz worked furiously during the closeout process to shave the cost overrun from its first estimate of nearly $1.7 million down to closer to $1.2 million, which has turned out to be manageable for us.

The building committee assumed a tight control of the process, meeting weekly to work through each closeout. The MRT board maintained a calm public face and we were spared the miseries of headlines and speculation in the press. In the calm wisdom of hindsight, a couple of members of our building committee have even reflected that a 10 percent cost overrun should not have been totally unexpected in a complex rehabilitation project.

It was an exhausting and trying time for all concerned. It was during this period that I began to develop unpleasant physical symptoms which I knew could really only be attributed to one of two things: stress or cancer. Once tests had alleviated my fears about cancer, my doctor insisted that I have a full physical. The results were predictable: overweight, high cholesterol and high blood pressure. He said, "What's going on here? You've always had blood pressure that was on the low side." All I could miserably offer as excuse was that I was undergoing enough stress to kill a water buffalo. Since then, diet and exercise have largely corrected the physical problems and as for the stress, well, one grows accustomed.

In the meantime, the calendar was moving forward. We finished the 1987-88 season, our first in the new building, with a surplus and the perception that the new building would perform as hoped for and, far from burying us as the nay-sayers had gleefully predicted, would give us some financial opportunities.

In July of 1988, the Wyndham Hotel opened on the northeast corner of the project, and in late August of 1988, the office tower was ready for occupancy, just about one year later than originally projected.

We entered the 1988-89 season with a full-blown case of "second-year slump." Subscriptions dropped back to an unusual low of 17,500, losing subscribers disgruntled by a season of construction dust, awkward access, and daring, controversial productions such as the MRT's collaboration with Arena Stage, StageWest and the Berkeley Rep on Tadashi Suzuki's production, *The Tale of Lear*, which opened in Milwaukee, played at the other three theatres, and wound up at a major international festival in Japan.

It was a tough season: subscriptions down, great difficulty creating public interest in the series in the Stackner Cabaret and Stiemke Theater, and generally negative audience response to the huge play from Chile, *The Torch*, which opened the season. Things began to improve as we premiered Romulus Linney's drama *Precious Memories* (now titled *Unchanging Love*), the building project problems began to come more under control, and I felt able to make a move that I had had to set aside the previous spring under the immediate shock of the discovery of the cost overrun.

I had intended to place a significant increase in marketing dollars in the 1988-89 budget. Now, at mid-year, I sought and won board authorization to increase expenditures for marketing, adding up to $55,000 during 1988-89, and $45,000 in 1989-90, drawing on our reserves if necessary to fund these expenditures.

With this money in hand, we set out to do more than shore up flagging sales for less-than-popular productions. We decided to also pump every advantage out of the popular productions. We had the seats, and set about selling them. This strategy was introduced with *Talley's Folly* and worked like a charm. To make a long story short, our total attendance for the year grew respectably; we did well financially and never needed to touch our reserves. The following season, ex-subscribers, frustrated at no longer finding the seats they wanted available, began to return to the fold.

This approach has since continued, and our marketing department has made great strides in the direction of both group and single-ticket sales. In the fourth season after opening, the Powerhouse series enjoyed a comfortable subscriber base of 18,700 and the Stackner Cabaret had, in the main, found its audience. The 198-seat Stiemke Theater remained the toughest nut to crack. Some of our most wonderful work is done during its four-play season, but our audience remains confused about its place in the general scheme of things. A new approach to selling its series was instituted for 1991-92 and time will tell. My early instinctive belief that it would take a minimum of five years after opening to really understand how best to operate our new facilities seems to be right on target.

But that second season was hard. I remember describing some of its difficulties to a colleague, who said reassuringly: "That's classic for the second season in a new home, isn't it?" "Yes," I blurted, "but it's happening to *me!*" Nevertheless, we again balanced our budget in that year.

Endgame

In the fall of 1988 came the opening of the Riverwalk; the fall of 1989 saw the installation of grand new banners along Wells Street, the opening of the Pabst Theater's marvelous new lobby combining both whimsicality and elegance, and

Liberty Bank's occupation of the remaining ground floor space in the newly named Milwaukee Center.

By the spring of 1989, new financial projections of the Rep's ability to appropriately meet its payments on the bond issue looked very good. The reduction of the construction overrun during the closeout period, decent interest rates, no draw upon our reserves, and pledge payments coming in with almost no delays had combined to give the MRT the prospect of skillfully using its own monies to pay off the debt and still retain a decent fiscal posture. These projections created relief all round and were, among other things, a tribute to the lack of panic and the patience exhibited in handling the original ugly financial surprise.

In the fall of 1990, revisions were made to the smoke-detector system, whose oversensitivity to the slightest dust in the air had given MRT staff and audience far too much practice in evacuating the building for false alarms.

The fall of 1990 also saw the installation of a new pediment on the Wells Street face of the building, thanks to a generous donation from the Todd Wehr Foundation. This completed the restoration of the exterior to its old grandeur and allowed us to finally declare complete the restoration/conversion of the old East Wells Power Plant into a new home for the Milwaukee Repertory Theater.

In January of 1992, the MRT retired the outstanding bond issue and emerged the free-and-clear owner of its facilities. The long road which opened before the Rep in 1978 had been walked to its completion.

Those long years were more to the Milwaukee Repertory Theater than a construction project. In the time since the MRT stepped out on the road to a new home, the theater company has also produced 141 plays, including 57 new American works or new translations as well as 15 revivals of *A Christmas Carol*; toured the Upper Midwest, adopted a formal policy of multicultural diversity and nontraditional casting, toured twice to Japan; participated in an international festival in Costa Rica; presented Japanese theater companies in the U.S.; sent its actors and directors to perform in Mexico, England and Japan; introduced its audiences to a range of work from Latin America, brought actors and directors to Milwaukee from every corner of the U.S. and Ireland, Mexico, England, Chile and Japan, and introduced several contemporary French plays to U.S. audiences. The MRT grew to be a home for playwrights Amlin Gray, Larry Shue, Romulus Linney, Maria Irene Fornes and John Leicht, and creators Ping Chong and Daniel Stein. The fifteen years will have added richness to our creative history, as well as new facilities in which to create.

And what did I learn? How to go without sleep or days off. How to be patient.

How to read the fine print. How to rely on the best people could give. How remarkable our staff really is. How extraordinary the power of this community on the move can be. How those with great power suffer from the same flaws, ego needs, jealousies and fears as the rest of us. The great satisfaction of sticking through to the end. The pleasure of working in a space *meant* to contain our company.

Would I do it again? No . . . but I don't need to, do I? And then, of course, there's the new long-range plan . . .

Postscript

In the spring of 1992, it's clear that the "Theater District Project" was a child of the high-rolling '80s. In the recession and real-estate slump of the '90s, Trammell Crow would be unable to contemplate such a project. Indeed, hard hit by large cost overruns, costly litigation against Morse/Diesel, cash-flow difficulties and their inability to rent up the office tower in a glutted market for office space, Trammell Crow is currently faced with a foreclosure suit by Teachers' Retirement System of Texas, their major lender. As for Morse/Diesel, they have closed their Milwaukee office.

The Milwaukee Repertory Theater, however, continues to operate comfortably in its quarters. Not that we are immune to the recession, but it is clear now that it was wise to be sole owners and operators of our spaces and captains of our own fate. Early on, the suggestion was made that somehow it would be better for Trammell Crow to control all the property, in the likelihood (then thought to be all too inevitable) that a little nonprofit organization like the Rep might go under and thereby jeopardize the development. We resisted, and as fate would have it, the big commercial entity is now the project participant that's overextended and staggering. Timing is everything.

Some people are in different places, too. For instance, Charles McNeer has retired as chairman of Wisconsin Electric. Mike Bolger has left the law firm to become president of the Medical College of Wisconsin. Frank Krejci, no longer with Briggs & Stratton, is vice-president of WITECH, Wisconsin Energy's venture capital arm. Bill Drew has left the Department of City Development for his own consulting firm. Beckley/Myers have several other theater projects behind them. Gina Spang is with Grunau Company and Jim Barron with Mortenson Construction. Donna

Meyer cochaired a recent $6-million campaign for the United Performing Arts Fund, and Larry Jost is current president of the board of the Milwaukee Repertory Theater.

As for the Milwaukee Repertory Theater, we are completing the seventeen productions of our 38th season and our fifth in the "new" home, and preparing to tour to Siberia in May.

S. O'C.
April 1992

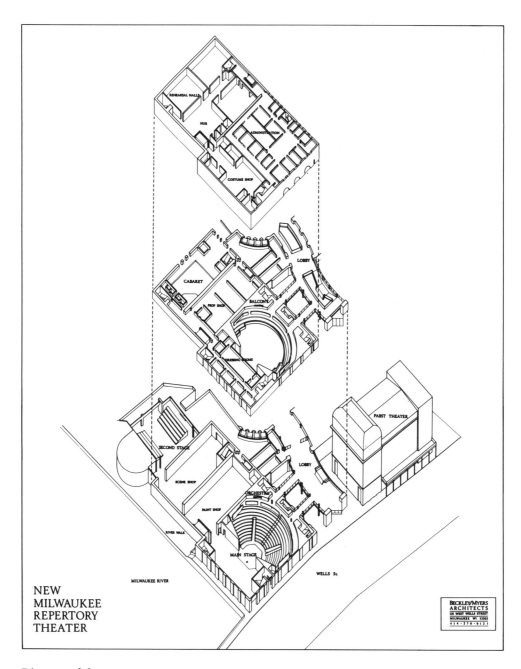

REHEARSAL HALLS

HUB

ADMINISTRATION

COSTUME SHOP

CABARET

LOBBY

PROP SHOP

BALCONY

DRESSING ROOMS

SECOND STAGE

PABST THEATER

SCENE SHOP

LOBBY

ORCHESTRA

PAINT SHOP

RIVER WALK

MAIN STAGE

MILWAUKEE RIVER

WELLS St.

NEW
MILWAUKEE
REPERTORY
THEATER

BECKLEY/MYERS
ARCHITECTS
125 WEST WELLS STREET
MILWAUKEE WI 53203
414·276·9121

Diagram of theater spaces.

PHILOSOPHY:

On Architecture

SHERRILL MYERS

Leon Battiste Alberti, the founding father of Italian Renaissance architecture, credited Vitruvius with defining three fundamental attributes of good architecture, firmness, commodity and delight. Although there are differences of emphasis among architects, the understanding of the need to reconcile multiple aspects of architecture has been with us a long time.

One of the fundamental challenges of architecture is the mandate to accomplish usability (commodity) while creating a work with esthetic merit (delight). The challenge occurs at the place where needs confront expression. If the collision between the two is creative, the architecture is enriched and the function is enhanced. If the resolution of this dichotomy occurs from a single viewpoint, either utilitarian or purely esthetic, the result is usually problematic. The resolution of these two aspects of architectural design requires dialogue and understanding. If the architect creates configurations and arrangements in isolation or in ignorance of function and usage, the result will likely be expressionistic in form and antagonistic in function. If on the other hand there is a high degree of understanding of the needs and the behavior of the users, the artistic expression can be accomplished while satisfying the need for utility.

A principle which guides our particular architectural firm is to create a synthesis between the best aspects of architectural theory and of architectural practice. Bob Beckley has been a member of academia since 1964 and I have been engaged in practice since about the same time, so there may be some question as to whether this is philosophical or pragmatic. In defense of the notion that this outlook comes about through conviction is the observation that many of the architects whose work we most admire have at some time or other been involved in teaching. The firm of Beckley/Myers Architects started as a partnership between Bob Beckley and myself while I was spending a year in Milwaukee as visiting professor at the University of Wisconsin-Milwaukee School of Architecture and Urban Planning, where Beckley was departmental chairman. That was my one and only full-time teaching experience and was no doubt more valuable to me than to my students. One of the important questions I learned to ask as a member of academia was "Okay, it works in practice, but does it stand up to theory?"

During the time I was teaching at the School of Architecture, there was a flourishing environmental behavioralist movement at UWM. Both Beckley and I taught some design studio courses with individuals from the "EBS" movement and were interested and influenced by their approach and by the literature in the field. A major emphasis was on designing so as to be responsive to human behavioral characteristics both anthropomorphic and psychological. Also, there was an emphasis on research activity and utilization of research findings. The Beckley/Myers assessment was that the research literature for the most part was soft and insubstantial whereas the approach and the underlying philosophy held a great deal of promise. My approach to teaching design studios at the university was to work directly with building users and surrogate client groups. Developing techniques to achieve a high degree of building user involvement in the design process seemed more promising to me than relying upon published research material as the basis for fundamental design decisions.

Beckley/Myers began the programming and design process for Milwaukee Repertory Theater with a high degree of commitment to creating usable facilities by using methods which enabled the members of the theater company to become actively involved in the design process. Some of these techniques were learned or tried out at UWM.

This pluralistic approach to planning extended to the formal aspects of the building design as well. We aimed for a building that would be reflective and expressive of a community of people. Not a building designed by committee, but a building that was complex in its expression. We did not harbor any notions of ending up with a building that was weak in its formal characteristics. The building had to inspire and uplift. It had to add dignity and style to the human activity it housed and it had to have handsome geometries. To accomplish this complexity of expression

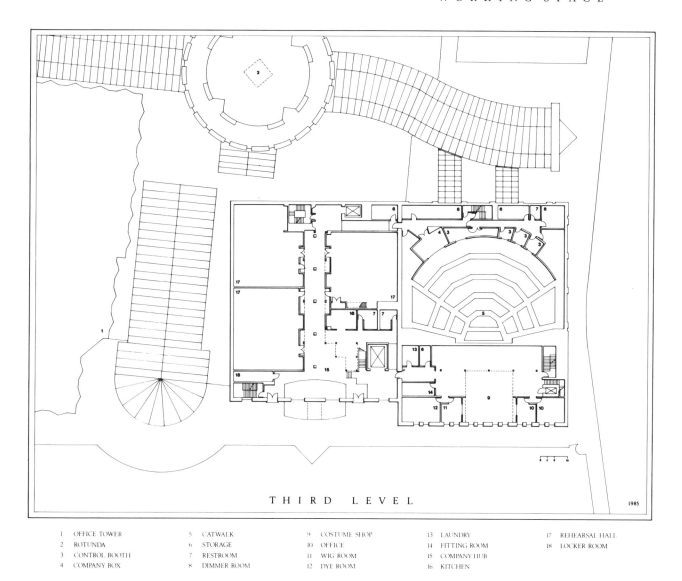

THIRD LEVEL

1985

1	OFFICE TOWER	5	CATWALK	9	COSTUME SHOP	13	LAUNDRY	17	REHEARSAL HALL
2	ROTUNDA	6	STORAGE	10	OFFICE	14	FITTING ROOM	18	LOCKER ROOM
3	CONTROL BOOTH	7	RESTROOM	11	WIG ROOM	15	COMPANY HUB		
4	COMPANY BOX	8	DIMMER ROOM	12	DYE ROOM	16	KITCHEN		

within our office we gave responsibility for the design of individual elements of the project to different individuals in the firm.

While Beckley/Myers were making a special effort to incorporate behavioral-science theory and research findings into the design process, the wider architectural community was also embarked upon a more eclectic course. A period had begun in which pluralism and complexity were displacing a narrow modernist dogmatism. Two influential additions to architectural writing at this time, for example, were Christopher Alexander's essay "A City is not a tree" and Robert Venturi's monograph

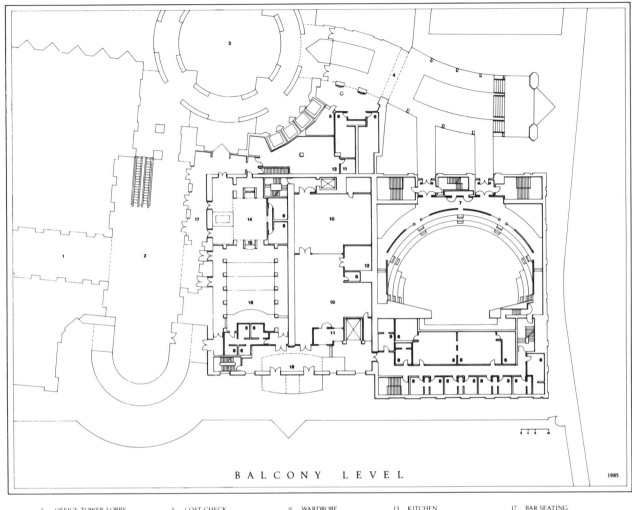

BALCONY LEVEL

1985

1	OFFICE TOWER LOBBY	5	COAT CHECK	9	WARDROBE	13	KITCHEN	17	BAR SEATING
2	ARBORETUM	6	RESTROOM	10	PROP SHOP	14	BAR	18	LOWER COMPANY HUB
3	ROTUNDA	7	BALCONY SEATING	11	OFFICE	15	CONTROL BOOTH		
4	LOBBY	8	DRESSING ROOM	12	CRAFT ROOM	16	CABARET		

"Complexity and Contradiction in Architecture." The postmodern movement in architecture became prominent during the period of this project. Another influence which I should acknowledge although he does not talk about architecture was William Barrett's book *The Illusion of Technique.* His definition of the characteristics of the post-Freudian intellect and the age of anxiety, as he terms it, suggested new avenues of artistic possibility to me. Central to this new possibility was the notion of the necessity of dealing creatively with fragments and incomplete elements. This type of artistic vision is found in the art of Laurie Anderson and Daniel Stein. Laurie

70

Anderson was one of the late-night music favorites at the Beckley/Myers studio on East Wells Street across the river from the future home of Milwaukee Rep.

Another factor which influenced our approach was a matter of pride. Time and again, we heard praise of building designers for creativity and style, but nothing but criticism of the ability of architects to design workable theater buildings. This criticism was especially intense where (backstage) theater support spaces were concerned. The Beckley/Myers team were determined to create a workable theater that held up to critical esthetic examination.

Milwaukee Repertory Theater: Philosophy & Culture

Had Beckley/Myers' outlook and approach not been sympathetic to pluralism and complexity, a working relationship with Milwaukee Rep would not have been sustainable. Philosophically MRT is a resident company, established to fulfill the artistic objectives which the regional theater movement established thirty or more years ago. Objectives such as artistic growth result from working in one place with one group of artists for a sustained period. The company functions as a self-sufficient, interdependent, creative ensemble. It is self-sufficient in the sense that everything necessary to produce a play, such as sets, costumes and props, is created within the walls of the theater. It is interdependent in that it is essential to have the coordination and cooperation of a number of artists, artisans, technicians and managers. The total number of employees in the company over the course of a season is around 200 people. For the theater to thrive and prosper, this diverse and numerous group of people must work together creatively and cooperatively.

Milwaukee Repertory Theater has a reputation as a very well-managed company. There are no successful regional theater companies that are not reasonably well managed. These companies have only one product and if that product fails there is nothing to carry them. Efficiency and effectiveness are not words you hear used in conversation at regional theater companies. They are too busy being efficient and too highly focused on being effective to talk about those attributes. One example will perhaps serve to illustrate the style of the managing director, Sara O'Connor. She tells staff members not to bring problems to her without potential solutions. The essence of good decision-making, she points out, is the availability of options to be made into decisions. It is the job of the managing director to make decisions. It is the job of staff to define options for decision-making.

How These Philosophies Meshed

The dialogue between the architects and the members of the theater company was animated, enthusiastic and purposeful. Because the company had labored so long under miserable working conditions there was a very high degree of interest in supporting the effort to define the attributes of an ideal theater. There was agreement among all the professional theater staff at Milwaukee Rep that theaters in the past had been designed with little or no regard to the people who worked in them. The architects gained the confidence of the theater company primarily because their commitment to changing this was recognized. There was a clear sense of mission and purpose which is essential for any successful project, but which is especially crucial when many individuals and disciplines are involved.

A technique that helped make the relationship work was the use of accessible open-door workshops. This was the primary method of working, and the workshops were conducted in the Rep's green room. The note cards, diagrams and sketches that were created during these workshops were left pinned to the wall. Since the green room was actually a wide area in the support-space passageway, these materials were very visible. This helped to underline the sense that the company as a whole was engaged in the planning process. The feeling was that the process was being carried out *with* the company rather than *for* the company. We believe that this is a crucial distinction. Also, Beckley and Myers conducted the workshops during hours that fit the theater schedule. Workshop sessions typically began in early evening and finished at performance time.

Two things should be acknowledged. The architects involved in the project did not invent the environmental behavior movement in architecture or the artistic outlook that made post-modernism possible. Furthermore, the realization that a good theater facility for a resident company had to include pleasant, safe, healthy and usable support facilities did not require original insight. What happened here was that some architects who were intensely interested in collaborative working, creative methodologies and user-friendly architecture met up with a client who was a creative, collaborative ensemble with a need for more space and a functional environment, and they clicked.

The Beckley/Myers outlook, which was sympathetic to pluralism and complexity, was a good fit with Milwaukee Rep's style. Perceived by the architects as a model for effective collaboration among diverse creative individuals, the MRT was both client and inspiration. This respect for the theater personnel resulted in an attitude on the part of the architects that acknowledged the theater company's expertise about things that were traditionally perceived to be within the architect's realm. Coupled with this outlook was the desire to establish a creative collaboration with the

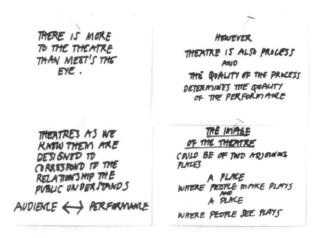

Architects' notes pinned up on the wall during workshops with theater staff.

individuals within the theater company. The principal tasks became, first of all, creating a structure for a dialogue between the theater company and the architects and a methodology for carrying the dialogue to a productive conclusion.

The Script (The Program):
The Process of Creating It

When we first became involved with MRT they were in a long-range planning mode and their facilities subcommittee asked us to give them some assistance in developing a strategy for examining the "facilities question." It was clear from the start that MRT's facilities were inadequate in many respects. They were cramped, ill lighted, poorly air-conditioned and inadequately ventilated. They were dispersed, the main 504-seat theater being located in a 1960s facility, the Milwaukee Performing Arts Center, designed to house multiple performing spaces for a variety of arts groups. A second studio-style theater, the Court Street Theater, was located about ten blocks away in a warehouse building where props were stored, rehearsals conducted and scenery painting carried out from time to time. It was in a neighborhood with a poor image. The facilities in the basement of the Performing Arts Center included a very inadequate scenery-construction shop, a costume shop and a rehearsal hall. The administrative offices were located four floors above in an exceedingly cramped space. Rehearsals were also conducted in local school gyms. The logistics of carrying out day-to-day operations was complex and time consuming. The balcony of the main theater had poor sightlines, the seating wrapped more than 180 degrees around the thrust stage, the backstage and dressing-room area was inadequate. There was a bizarre lighting-grid-trapeze-net contraption over the stage, seat spacing was excessively close and there were fewer seats than the Rep needed.

The need for improvement was easy to see. The primary questions were, "Could new facilities be constructed for an affordable cost?" "Had constructing new facilities been a successful enterprise for other similar companies?" Each of these rather large questions had a subset of other questions. It was not possible for us to answer these questions adequately without more evidence than we could find after carrying out a fairly exhaustive literature search. It was apparent that there had been a number

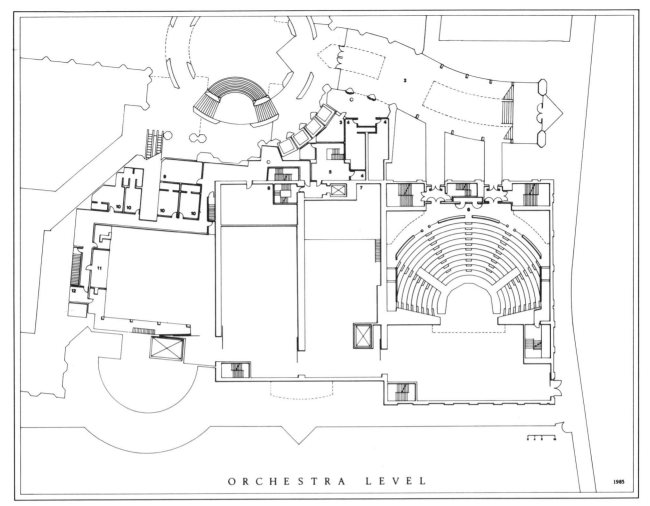

ORCHESTRA LEVEL

1985

1	ROTUNDA	5	WORKROOM	9	GREENROOM
2	LOBBY	6	MAIN STAGE SEATING	10	DRESSING ROOM
3	COAT CHECK	7	UPPER PAINT SHOP	11	CONTROL BOOTH
4	RESTROOM	8	MECHANICAL	12	DIMMER ROOM

of (then) recent projects which were known to theater people but which had received very little attention in the professional architectural press. And although there were rumors and stories of success and failures there was very little hard analytical information.

As a result of a grant from the NEA we were able to commence a study titled "Theater Facility Impact Study" to find answers to these questions. We set out to prepare a set of guidelines for planning performing-art facilities which would have general applicability together with specific guidelines and strategies for Milwaukee Rep.

We proposed a framework for analyzing theater consisting of four types of considerations: performing, operations, audience and economic. The idea was that

75

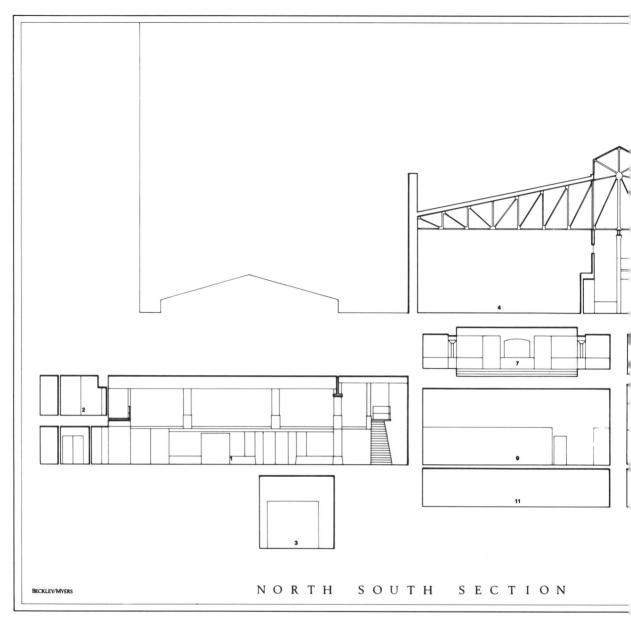

NORTH   SOUTH   SECTION

1	2ND STAGE	5	UPPER COMPANY HUB
2	CONTROL BOOTH	6	COMPANY HUB
3	LOADING DOCK	7	CABARET
4	REHEARSAL HALL	8	PROP SHOP

these four categories would form the basis for discussing theater needs and attributes, making it possible for a dialogue to occur that crossed departmental boundaries. This framework gave the architects an effective role immediately, as facilitator of the dialogue among individuals from different disciplines within the theater in an exploration of the four topics.

A series of workshops were held focusing on these four areas. In the workshops

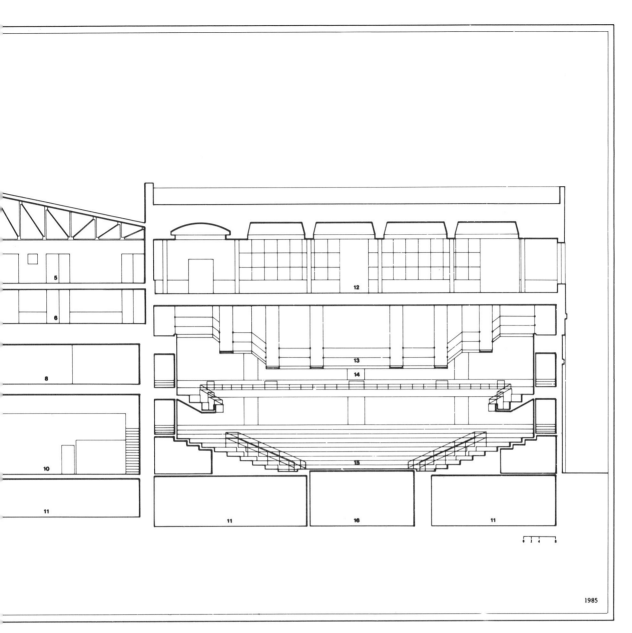

1985

9	SCENE SHOP	13	CATWALK
10	PAINT SHOP	14	BALCONY SEATING
11	STORAGE	15	MAIN STAGE
12	ADMINISTRATION	16	TRAP ROOM

there were discussions about goals, facts, needs, issues, strategies and options. The architects did virtually all the preparation of materials, props, agendas and so on to prepare for the workshops and then prepared the follow-up notes and summaries. The initial workshops were very free ranging although the agenda was always followed. For example, a discussion could begin with consideration of goals that applied to the topic area, say operations. If someone wanted to jump to a discussion of needs or of important issues that should be addressed, the discussion was allowed to range. It was always the (architect) facilitator's job to keep track of the information offered and to cover the entire topic. There were at least two sessions for each topic.

Session one covered goals, facts, needs and issues. Between sessions one and two more facts were gathered from individuals. Session two explored strategies and options for satisfying the needs and meeting the goals defined earlier. The architects brought prepared suggestions to the sessions to serve as a means of stimulating discussion, and exploring potential directions. Abbreviated notes and key words were written down on 4″×6″ cards as the discussions progressed and pinned up on the wall so that the theater people were able to see how the architects were interpreting

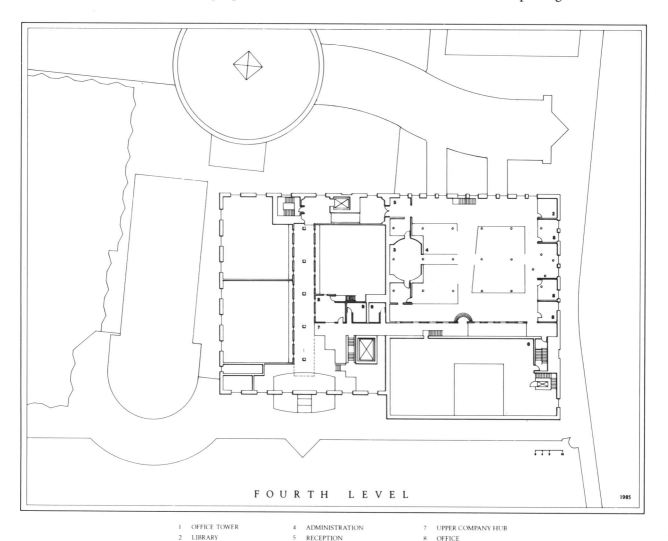

FOURTH LEVEL

1985

1	OFFICE TOWER	4	ADMINISTRATION	7	UPPER COMPANY HUB
2	LIBRARY	5	RECEPTION	8	OFFICE
3	BOARD ROOM	6	COSTUME STORAGE	9	RESTROOM

what they were hearing. In this manner it was possible to deal with misunderstandings and misconceptions immediately. The emphasis in the workshops was on defining attributes of the "Ideal Theater," defining what worked and did not work in the present facilities and other people's theater facilities, and finding out what lessons had been learned elsewhere that should be disseminated and improved upon in Milwaukee. The Ideal Theater was not considered to be a "Gold Plated Theater" or a "Rolls Royce Theater" but rather an effective and supportive theater. There was no encouragement to fantasize about a "Perfect Theater" or to create a wish list just to work off steam.

We used three techniques to gather information and develop an understanding about the company's needs and parameters: group workshops, individual interviews and questionnaires.

The workshops were open to anyone in the company who was interested in the particular topic or in how his or her area of concern was affected by the topic. Anyone could come to a discussion about economics or operations and fortunately people did, to gain an understanding of how those considerations would affect decisions about the planning and design of the facilities. Virtually all disciplines were represented to some degree. The result was the creation of an overall definition of the issues by a cross section of the company and by a large number of individuals. Our impression at the time was that a good general understanding of needs and priorities was developed. Though the process may have had very little or nothing to do with it, we noted an absence of competitiveness or jealousy between departments during the design process.

Individual interviews and work sessions were used to gather and define detailed information about all the aspects of the company's operations and activities. We worked with groups and individuals representing

□ Artistic direction

□ Administration and management

□ Production

□ Stage management

□ Actors

□ Costume design and construction

- ☐ Scenery design and construction

- ☐ Scenery painting

- ☐ Theater technology—lighting, rigging and staging

The third format for information-gathering was the questionnaire worksheet. It had blanks for specific types of information as well as an open part for comments. We also received copies of articles and excerpts from books which individuals considered valuable, as well as some sketches and diagrams representing ideal configurations, dimensions and so on. A looseleaf binder was kept in the architect's office for this material and an identical copy was maintained at the MRT.

The Ideal Theater Model

The idea of a model was to create a diagram which would define the important attributes of a theater conceived to enhance artistic, operational, audience and economic aspects of MRT. The model primarily dealt with proximities and relationships, and revealed a fundamental dilemma at the outset of planning: everything needs to be near everything else. The process of creating a diagram using paper cutouts (with members of the company) revealed that it was geometrically impossible for everything to be adjacent to everything else. It was fairly easy to move on to considerations of getting from place to place within the theater and to the realization that movement was another crucial factor. We recognized that we needed a concept for accomplishing good communications within the facilities. Nothing is more crucial in the process of architectural planning and design than the development of a clear organizing concept. The first such concept to emerge from the workshops resulted from the notion that the rehearsal function is the primary organizing activity in the process of creating theater. The concept we developed was of a village square where the entire life of the theater community crossed paths outside the doors of the rehearsal halls. This concept came about as a result of an archetypal design-research question: "What is the heart of your theater?"

This space was named "the Hub" by John Dillon to describe another characteristic it should have. It should be the hub of activity. Further discussion of this

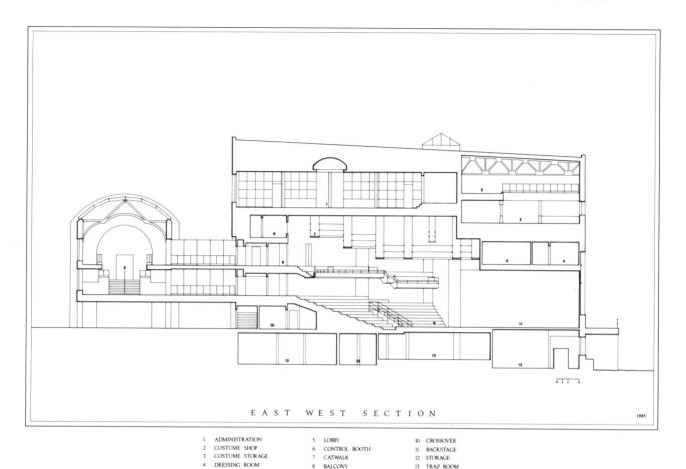

EAST WEST SECTION

1985

1	ADMINISTRATION	5	LOBBY	10	CROSSOVER
2	COSTUME SHOP	6	CONTROL BOOTH	11	BACKSTAGE
3	COSTUME STORAGE	7	CATWALK	12	STORAGE
4	DRESSING ROOM	8	BALCONY	13	TRAP ROOM
		9	MAIN STAGE		

notion led to the observation that although company members would recognize the Hub as an appropriate heart of the theater, the audience would regard the theater's house as the heart. The model for MRT which developed established two distinct zones of activity and influence, the public and the semiprivate.

The theater was considered to be an urban institution and it was regarded as important that it have a public face and that it engage the life of the city. The concept of a "public place" was formulated to define a place which the theater would share with commercial activities. The place where the hubbub of the city rubbed against the theater.

81

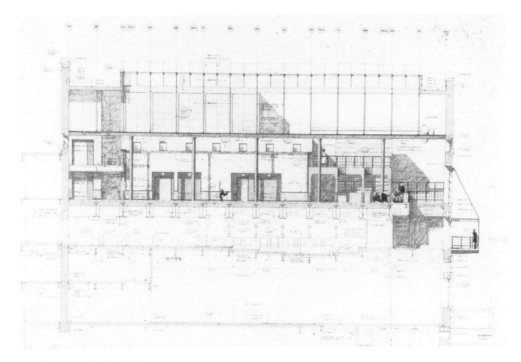

Section through the Hub.

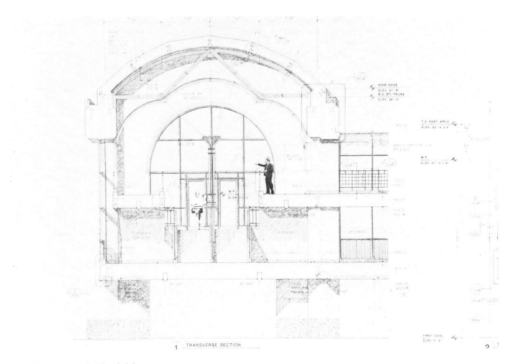

Section through the lobby.

The Real Thing:
Applying The Guidelines and
Ideal Model to the Power Plant

There were two quite distinct parts of the theater facilities project. One was creating the "Theater District" master plan for a mixed-use development, which was used to attract a developer to the project. This developer, the Trammell Crow Company, subsequently carried out, in modified form, the commercial parts of the master plan: a hotel, office building and galleria. The second part, designing the theater, was carried out within the framework of the master plan and involved considerable interface with the developer's space. There is actually some physical overlap of spaces at different levels requiring air rights, easements and lease arrangements. This necessitated a great deal of interaction and coordination between Beckley/Myers and the developer's architects, Skidmore Owings and Merrill. This occurred both in negotiating their development of the master plan and in working out the interface issues resulting from our design of the theater. We would like to acknowledge the excellent working relationship we enjoyed with SOM and with Trammell Crow vice president Jon Hammes.

In the part of the study devoted to MRT's need, we evaluated four existing buildings and three possible new construction sites as potential homes for Milwaukee Rep. Although each of the alternatives was considered to be potentially available, there were conditions attached to the availability of each one. We were not in the process of finding a site at that time. We were in the process of demonstrating how to evaluate a site. Of these alternatives the East Wells Street Power Plant was somewhat more compelling than any of the others and considerably more compelling than some. There were shortcomings nevertheless, and one of the tasks we ultimately faced was to overcome the problems inherent in converting a structure of such a different type into a working theater.

The principal advantages which the power plant offered were:

☐ A highly visible location in close proximity to other familiar performing arts facilities.

☐ A large clear span space in the plant's old turbine room which was adequate for a 700-hundred seat thrust-stage auditorium.

☐ Excess land which could be sold to a developer to generate capital for the construction of the theater.

The principal problems were:

☐ Major expense for demolition. (The buildings were full of huge items of equipment and boilers which had to be cut into pieces for removal.)

☐ Considerable unknowns insofar as the buildings' structure and condition were concerned. (The buildings consisted of three structures, two of which were retained for the theater. Both were in excess of 80 years old and, being filled with equipment, were extremely difficult to measure and evaluate.)

☐ No front door. (The only workable configuration of audience-stage resulted in the existing front facade of the building becoming the side of the rehabilitated building.)

☐ Nonalignment of floors. (None of the floors lined up in the two buildings which were rehabilitated.)

☐ The expense of making openings through the huge structural masonry walls.

The major planning decisions were strongly affected by the disposition of space within the existing buildings. The two connected (and oldest) buildings were retained for converting into theater facilities. The building which faced onto the principal street was well suited for use as the main theater, and the adjoining building, which was primarily a workshop for the boiler plant, was converted into theater shops and other support spaces. Although the configuration we proposed in the guidelines envisaged a lobby for the main theater in a space overlooking the river, the theater district master plan called for the lobby to be connected to the public galleria. Providing public access to all the buildings comprising the theater district, the galleria was to be located in an abandoned street which ran parallel to the river on the opposite side of the mainstage building. This plan resulted in the former boiler room alongside the river becoming a very large backstage area. The turbine room, because

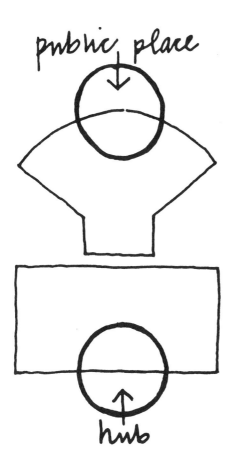

Concept diagram.

of its large free-span open area, was conceived as the auditorium in both plans. The first plan had a lobby attached to the east wall of the turbine room. The lobby faced onto a small plaza, set back from East Wells Street. Also facing onto this plaza was the south entrance into the galleria. As a result of historic preservation considerations the lobby design was changed to create a lobby above this small plaza detached from the facade of the turbine room. All this probably sounds complex. The point is that considerations of the relationship to other buildings within the master plan, and historic-preservation considerations, had a major influence on fundamental planning decisions for the theater. An important question is whether the influence was good or detrimental to the theater. I believe that the influences were good in both instances. The lobby is more attractive as a result of being detached from the facade of the historic structures, and the connection of the lobby to the public galleria space is clearly advantageous to the theater. This suggests to me that theaters needn't be islands. Also it suggests that, in the urban setting, the more intimate the connections between buildings are the more appealing they are to the public. By contrast it is

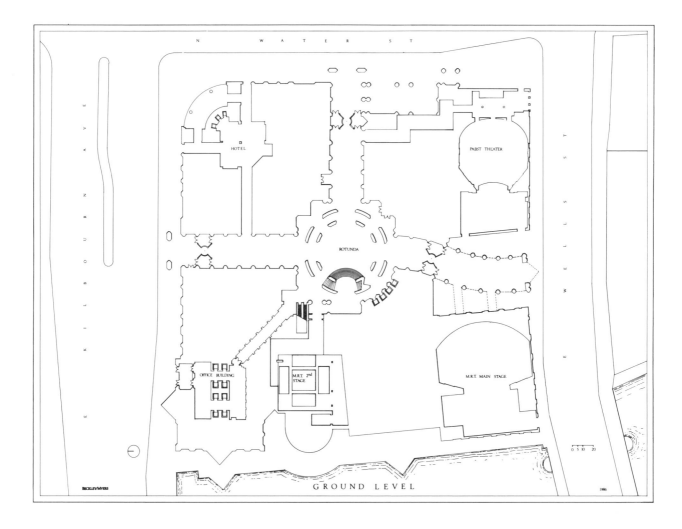

impossible to avoid the impression that the Performing Arts Center, which is across the street from the new Milwaukee Rep, is a fortress.

The building adjoining the turbine room was usable for scenery and paint-shop purposes, and its upper floors became the shell for the rehearsal halls. Also a space overlooking the river in this structure became the Hub.

In addition to considerations of utilizing existing spaces for their most appropriate functions, there were other guiding principles. One was ideal proximities of different functions. A great deal of time was spent with members of the company discussing working relationships and which functional groups needed more immediate access to each other. Another was to utilize distance to help reduce conflicts between noisy activities and those needing quiet. The rehearsal halls were placed at the furthest end of things. A third was to organize functions in zones that had similar environmental needs. Dirty activities next to dirty, clean next to clean. These working principles helped reduce our dependence upon expensive technologies.

Our technique for the planning and design of the spaces in the theater involved review by theater personnel at every step in the process. My role as partner-in-charge was to keep the individual designers headed in the same direction and to act as the eyes and ears of the theater company in our shop.

In designing a building, most architects follow a series of five steps defined by the American Institute of Architects as basic services: schematic design, design development, construction documentation, bidding and construction. Schematic design is conceptual in nature; it defines the major elements, massing and configuration of things. It establishes proximities and functional relationships. During the design development phase all the major systems—structural, heating and ventilating, and so on—are integrated into the design scheme. Primary dimensions are determined and the design is more fully refined in function and esthetics. The construction document phase is the period when the specifications and drawings to be used for construction purposes are prepared. The bidding phase involves the steps in obtaining bids from construction companies. The construction phase is exactly what it sounds like and is just as dynamic and challenging as you may have heard.

In our firm we operate differently in only a couple of respects. We believe very firmly that basic services should include programming and that the practice of commencing design without a properly defined program is the single greatest reason for unsatisfactory buildings of all sorts. In the simplest terms it is like trying to cook without a recipe, which may be fine for scrambled eggs but not for Eggs Benedict.

Another significant difference, we believe, concerns ideas of what should occur during the design development phase. This period should be used to refine and develop the quality of the design and all truly good architects do this. However, it appears to be common to use design development to incorporate technology and systems and to prepare a set of dimensioned documents which can be handed over to construction draftsmen without the objective of taking the design to a higher level of quality.

It is necessary during the design development phase to have highly detailed working sessions with all the engineering and specialist disciplines to incorporate building and environmental systems and to coordinate all the components and elements of the building. It is tempting to keep the people who will be using and operating the theater at arm's length during this period and just develop the schematic design to the next level of completeness. Once an engineer or an architect has, through hard work and long hours, arrived at a technically sound solution to some aspect of the building design, it is very difficult to get them to change to suit the desires of the owners and users. It is difficult for emotional and financial reasons. If you have to do something twice, you make less money. However, the users have made decisions during schematic design which are schematic in nature. They need to be involved in the decision-making process during design development along with the architects and engineers.

During the construction document phase the architects and engineers are in the process of preparing the drawings and specifications which individual construction-trades people will use to carry out their role in the physical construction of the building. The drawings for this purpose are more technical in nature than the design development drawings, and considerably more detailed. It is very common for the building owner and users to be virtually quarantined from this part of the process. However, it is necessary during this phase to have thorough working sessions with the people who will be using and operating the theater to work out as many of the bugs as possible.

What We Learned

If we compare our experience designing Milwaukee Rep to designing other theaters and facilities, a number of things stand out. First, working with theater people can result in a highly creative collaboration. Second, effective utilization of the technical expertise contained within resident performing arts companies can shorten the decision-making loop and result in a higher level of quality. Third, mature, experienced theater companies (should) have the capability to define their facility needs and parameters, with good assistance, to a higher level than is possible for less experienced and less technically substantial companies. It is important for companies to understand both their strengths and their weaknesses in this regard.

The economic challenge which we set at the outset of the project, to make facilities an asset rather than a liability, served to stimulate the creation of a mixed-use project, although the particulars worked out somewhat differently than originally imagined. The example we pointed to in the guidelines, the Museum of Modern Art project, was an inspiration. The theater district project had to be developed within the economic, social and political framework of Milwaukee. Part of that framework was the successful experience in Milwaukee of carrying out a major downtown retail redevelopment project a few blocks away and just prior to launching this project. That project, The Grand Avenue, was an inspired example of public-private cooperative development which became the foundation for carrying out the theater district project. The strength of the public-private partnership in Milwaukee became one of the single greatest assets upon which Milwaukee Rep was able to draw.

We found that estimates of operating costs proved fairly accurate; however, estimating the economic performance of restaurants and bars is not as predictable. The evidence is still not in on the profitability of the cabaret food and drink operations.

You would probably not expect to be able to take a new musical instrument out of its box and perform perfectly with it immediately. This may not be the most appropriate analogy, but you need to tune and adjust a theater and learn its characteristics before you can get the most from it. It may not be possible to have all the time you would like to do this, so prepare your audience.

We did not set out to build a perfect theater and we did not build a perfect theater. All the mistakes we made as designers could have been avoided but no one can avoid making any mistakes. With reasonable diligence and luck you will spot most of them when they can be rectified, before construction is complete.

Provide a generous contingency as part of your budget. If rehab is involved, provide an even more generous contingency. If construction management is utilized, get a guaranteed maximum price.

It is important to carry out a process of thorough critical review from design through construction so that the decisions made at one step are carried through at the next. Inevitably, as the project progresses and more individuals become involved, variations in interpretation occur. This is only human; however, the problem has to be overcome. The objective is to utilize these differences of insight, interpretation and opinion creatively rather than accidentally.

Powerhouse Theater.

Afterword

JOHN DILLON

I remember my first visit to Gettysburg. I was struck by the beauty of the place: the well-manicured meadows, the scenic vistas, vacationers picnicking in the shade of trees in full leaf. The battlefield, of course, took on a very different look as, armed with a guidebook and my imagination, I envisioned the horrible events that took place here one hot July in 1863.

That visit came to mind as I read Sara's account of the bloodless battles that led to the creation of our new complex. Visitors to our new facility all seem suitably impressed by what we wrought, but those of us who lived through the building process (or who are armed with Sara's "guidebook") can walk through the structure, and see the roof of the lobby and remember "The Copper Roof Wars," or walk the Riverwalk and recall how its construction costs could have broken us fiscally, and on and on.

In fact, one of the things I enjoy most about our new home is just how easy and pleasurable it is *to* walk through. The creative act is never easy. One constantly battles lack of will, lack of imagination, lack of money. The least your building should do for you is make your job easier, not be another barrier to overcome as you strive for excellence. In our old home, a stroll through various workstations was an impossibility; so, too, the chance to drop in on your comrades and see how the construction of a set or the pace of rehearsals was proceeding. Instead, it meant keys and doorways, slow elevators and car rides. Today, because of the careful planning we did, I can almost instantly see who's at their desks on the fifth floor and a short flight of steps takes me down to the company booth where I can watch a bit of a technical rehearsal or check in on a difficult scene during a matinee performance without disturbing anyone. This booth, on the same level as the stage manager's booth, allows directors to converse with designers and playwrights during a preview performance. Lately, the booth has also become popular for company members' spouses with new infants (we've been having quite a baby boom around here of late), since a crying child can't disturb the performance down below. You can even park a nervous director in it on opening night, hand him or her a bottle of scotch and open up the wet bar. I guess you could call it our own "skybox."

Continuing down the corridor brings you past the rehearsal halls. Their sliding black curtains allow stage managers to restructure the space and allow actors (or an artistic director who's paying a short visit) to slip in and out of the room unnoticed. Past the rehearsal halls lies "the Hub," that common area meant to bring our company together just like the village green of old.

If I continued this verbal tour, floor-by-floor, I could explain how each work-space, designed in consultation with the people destined to work in it, not only fits the needs of those who use it, but also illustrates elements of the artistic philosophy of the company that occupies it.

The building, in short, is a concrete reminder of the MRT's operating assumptions. To understand the true meaning of that statement, we have to go back to the long-range planning process and see how, I believe, it led us to do the most crucial thing we had to do: Ask the right questions.

"The questions you ask determine the answers you get." It was the most important lesson I learned in my college Soc. Stat. class. If we'd simply asked "what do we need in a new building," our only answers would have been architectural. But the long-range planning process asked who are we? What do we strive to do? What will help us to do that better? And that, in turn, led us to build explicit and implicit assumptions of our troupe's work right in there with the mortar and brick, metal and glass. Openness, accessibility, ease of communication, these are some of the things we value in our work together, and that Beckley and Myers turned into a superb theater plant. For example, the "Hub" also reflects the openness of the company, of trying to promote the idea of our being a theatrical family. Likewise, office spaces were made as "out in the open" as possible. Where a solid wall might have stood in my office, there's a wall of glass. It allows sunlight to carry through from the two large windows in my room and spread throughout the administrative area. But, more important, it means everyone can see when I'm in as they pass by, encouraging them to pop in to discuss

Stackner Cabaret.

matters large and small. Likewise, it makes it easier for me to share an idea with an actor, a director, a technician.

The actor is at the heart of our art at the MRT and we wanted that reflected in our performance spaces. A thrust stage is, I believe, where the actor can be most central to the dramatic event. While our new mainstage, the Powerhouse, allowed better sightlines and thus more opportunities for designers, we still wanted to keep the actor as close to the audience as possible. The Stiemke, with only 200 seats, ensures the performer intimacy no matter how the seats are arranged, and the 100-seat Stackner Cabaret has been especially helpful in stretching the performance muscles of our actors by giving some of them their first opportunity to work in a space where they must fully acknowledge the presence of the audience.

Returning to the design of the Powerhouse, in light of our policy of openness, designing our own theater meant we could build in assumptions about ticket prices as well, as we could design the auditorium to be sectioned off in certain ways. Critical to this was our desire to have a theater that was open to all, to always have good seats available at admission prices comparable to the movies.

As I mentioned earlier, a chief goal was getting architecture to help, not hinder us. Our building project was intended not to force us to change our work but to enable us to do our work better. (Since some of our work had been, and would continue to be, controversial, I remember a comical afternoon when Sara and I practiced rising swiftly from various styles of theater seats to see which ones banged closed with the least amount of noise, anticipating those plays that might drive the faint-hearted from the theater.) And that's why as much care (and expense) went into workspaces as into the auditoriums themselves. Anyone contemplating a new theater will find themselves, like us, involved in a dialectic with our aspirations for the future and a confrontation with the present building, with its limitations and strengths. Certainly, the work we did studying other theaters was crucial in expanding the range of possibilities open to us. But the main influences, as I said, were the good and bad points of the old space. This led us into one trap, for the things that weren't part of our former life in the Performing Arts Center were hardest to prepare for. Details like equipment for the Powerhouse lobby bar, or storage space for the janitorial staff, were all new needs we could have better anticipated. And while we vastly improved sightlines, designers and directors still have to be careful to accommodate patrons viewing the play from the balcony and extreme sides of the orchestra. Nor were we completely successful in designating a location for sign-language interpreters or anticipating all the support space we'd need for the expanded artistic, technical and administrative staff needed to create fifteen new productions each season (plus our annual revival of *Christmas Carol*).

What's important is that we dared to dream of the "Ideal Theater," that we were able to ask the big, challenging questions and not hurriedly solve a real-estate emergency. For that opportunity to "thing big," full thanks goes to the MRT's board of directors, as well as for their commitment to fully collaborate with our artists, artisans, technicians and administrative staff in that process.

I was visiting with a fellow artistic director recently who'd also experienced the ordeal of creating a new theatrical home. He admitted that both the excitement and the pressure of the process had made the artistry of the troupe during those seasons take a back seat. The result: The company had arrived in their new home artistically crippled and it would take him years to rebuild the troupe and its work habits so that its artistry matched the excellence of its new surroundings.

Early in our process we realized such a pitfall could be fatal for us and that, therefore, while I would be working closely on the design of the new building, I wouldn't have as many of those popular 7:30 A.M. meetings as Sara would, my involvement in fund-raising would be minimized when possible, etc. In other words, my primary job remained the same, to make sure each production would strive after the greatest possible artistic quality just as we strove to create the highest level of quality possible in our new home. The aim (and, I hope, the result) was to bring the finest artistic team possible to center stage on October 22, 1987. Which brings me to the bottom line, the one ingredient most needed to make an undertaking like our building project succeed. It's really quite simple: Besides a dedicated board and a foresighted president, a supportive community and gifted architects, you need a managing director with the dedication, tireless energy, attention to endless detail, and vision of a Sara O'Connor. She not only negotiated all the rapids and climbed all the mountains, she also protected our artistry at each step of the way. The building, and the work we do in it, will always stand as a testament to her and her lifelong contribution to the art of theater in this country. My debt to her is too great to ever repay, but at least let me acknowledge it here.

THE SPACE IN USE:

Comments From the Company

The new home of the MRT far exceeds anything I was capable of imagining during the process. The facility is indeed conducive to creativity and provides a wonderfully encouraging atmosphere for our work. As an actor and director, it has been a delight to dine on the creative culinary treats of our three stages and to experience the attendant periods of excitement, frustration and satisfaction that come with such acquaintances.

Kenneth Albers
Associate Artistic Director

THE SPACE IN USE:

Comments From the Company

We only moved across the street, but we transformed ourselves from subterranean termites into seagulls. We used to work in the basement of the Performing Arts Center, where there was no natural light, no space, no fresh air. The environment was deadening. Now we work on the fourth floor of a grand old recycled Victorian building where we can see the light and the sky change, where we can watch the Milwaukee River flow, where we can open a window to breathe fresh air, and, like those seagulls, see the topmost façades of our neighbor buildings respond to the changing seasons. What a place to allow our imaginations to soar!

Rose Pickering
Actor

THE SPACE IN USE:

Comments From the Company

Since the design for the Marketing/PR Department is similar to past quarters, but on a larger scale, the most dramatic shifts came about with the inclusion of space for computer equipment. This new tool has enabled our in-house production to expand tenfold, and in a curious way has allowed our programming to move ahead with the same feeling of freedom that natural light brings to a workspace.

The open-door policy that is encouraged at the MRT and is facilitated by the layout of our area (absence of doors and full walls) is at times distracting, since PR traditionally is a high-traffic area, due to the nature of the work. To counterbalance this, the new facility has provided many areas where more privacy can be obtained.

Unfortunately, these private areas are slowly becoming our storage areas, due to rapid growth and our ever-increasing needs.

Fran Serlin-Cobb
Marketing & Public Relations Director

THE SPACE IN USE:

Comments From the Company

Long before our move, I consulted with other shop managers, visited several new shops to get ideas and information, and discussed ideal work spaces and conditions with my shop. With our wish list in hand, the costume staff went to meet with the architects. Eventually we were told that we would have the prime 4th-floor river-view space. Then the exciting work began, of making this space work for us, planning equipment, storage units and work spaces, and adjusting the wish list to the physical and financial limitations.

In the summer of '87, I donned overalls, workboots and a hard hat and with the other tech department heads helped build and install costume storage units and move equipment and storage into our new spaces. After two-and-a-half seasons, we are still adjusting lighting to suit our needs and using rubber mats to cushion the vinyl-covered cement floor, but the improvement in working space and equipment and atmosphere has increased our efficiency and enjoyment of costuming.

Sometimes I feel almost guilty about having such a wonderful shop to work in—but then I think how hard we worked to get it, and how awful our old space was, and I know we deserve it.

Diane B. Dalton
Costume Shop Supervisor